D0910936

The Real Life 101 Handbook

Handbook

A BEGINNER'S GUIDE TO THE WORLD AFTER HIGH SCHOOL

BY

MIKE DURALIA

authorHOUSE®

AuthorHouse™
1663 Liberty Drive, Suite 200
Bloomington, IN 47403
www.authorhouse.com
Phone: 1-800-839-8640

First published by AuthorHouse   1/5/2009

ISBN: 978-1-4343-7626-8 (sc)

Printed in the United States of America
Bloomington, Indiana

This book is printed on acid-free paper.

For my daughter Emily:
*I hope that your life becomes for you the beautiful
reflection of the truly wonderful spirit that is uniquely you!*

Contents

Preface

THE WORLD was a different place before September 11, 2001. As we watched in horror as the two towers burned and eventually crumbled we were all reminded that life is a precious gift and the time we have here is limited. You never know what can happen. You can never completely plan for the unexpected because by definition you do not know exactly for what you should prepare. During the days, weeks, months and years following that horrible event, many Americans reflected upon the meaning of their lives, realigned their life priorities and made a commitment to do the things they always wanted to do but for whatever reason had not accomplished. I was one of those people and this book is my contribution to help make the world a better place.

How often do you ask yourself "Why am I here?" or "What is *my* purpose in life?" Unfortunately, there is no book available where you can flip to the page with your name on it and read exactly what it is you are supposed to do with your life. I do know this; if you allow your mind to become clear and you sit quietly long enough the little voice inside you that you are rarely able to hear when the world is buzzing around you will give you the answer.

The trouble is if you are like me, you did not have time to slow down long enough to listen. We are all too busy doing to just "be" and contemplate those larger questions of life. In many ways that is a tragedy but there is good news – you have total control over that situation. You can decide to slow down and listen and you decide, you alone, what you want to do with your life. There were several major events that happened in my life in the few months following 9/11 that finally made me stop. And think. And listen. The result of that introspection was the idea for this book.

I have always had a knack for teaching. I have earned two degrees; one in engineering and one in business. Throughout my academic career I found I was always helping my classmates understand the complicated material we were being taught. Somehow, I was able to put it all into simple terms so anyone and everyone could understand. That truly is my purpose in life. That is why I am here. I have always done it at school, at work, with my kids, with my family and friends – always. Now, I am doing it for a much larger group in the hopes that I may pass along to you some wisdom I have gained during my short time on this planet.

I am not a professor. I am not a financial genius. I am not offering to sell you something that will help you get rich in 3 weeks or less if you only send me $2,000 of your hard earned money. What I can offer is some information that you most likely have never seen previously. Hopefully, you will learn some things that will help you avoid some of the major mistakes I made earlier in my life. I made those mistakes because I did not know what I did not know. I know more now and I realize that you can never stop learning. If you are always seeking knowledge, you will continue to have the life you want; the life you deserve. Mao Zedong, the former leader of the People's Republic of China once said, "Complacency is the enemy of study. We cannot really learn anything until we rid ourselves of complacency." While I may not agree with most of the man's ideas, wiser words were never spoken. Take them to heart.

This book is primarily intended for high school students who are fast approaching graduation and are not aware yet of the challenges they will face but the information in it will be helpful to anyone who wants to learn more about personal finance. Again, you don't know what you don't know. If you're about to graduate, you've spent 12 years being "educated" and you will soon find out that you learned a lot of good information but you do not have all the tools you need to succeed in your life. When you go to buy your first car, you will not have to do any Algebra but you will need to understand the Time Value of Money equation if you want to be able to calculate your payments. But what is the best way to buy a new car? How will you pay for it? How much will the insurance cost? Can you afford the taxes? These and many other questions we will answer as we move through the Chapters. So find a quiet place, open your mind and get ready to receive the information you should have already been given.

Introduction

IT'S STRANGE how we educate people in this country. Most folks agree that our education system needs to be revamped yet very little has been done to change it. Groups have suggested vouchers, privatization, standardized testing and a whole host of other ways to make the educational system better. Unfortunately, no one has addressed the real problem; a lot of the information taught in school today is not applicable to real life.

In spite of that, there is a lot of good in our schools. We teach our children how to add and subtract, read and write, the history of our great country and the basics of science and economics to help prepare them for life as an adult. Nevertheless, most kids graduate high school without the ability to balance a checkbook. They are unaware of what is really involved with buying their first car or home (knowing the terms of the Louisiana Purchase is not going to help them get the best deal on either one). They are not taught how to find a job and, once they do, are surprised at the amount of taxes taken out of their first paycheck. We leave them to learn these lessons on their own and oftentimes the lessons are quite costly. Since we do not provide any real guidance in these areas, why is it so surprising that the upon graduation the average college student has over $4,000 of credit card debt and the average American $8,500?

My parents did a pretty good job of teaching me the value of money. When I desired a particular thing, they did not just run out and buy it for me. I had to work for it, save my money and wait until I could afford it. They gave me a credit card to use in college and carefully monitored how I used it and made sure I could pay it off every month. However, we did not discuss their financial situation in our home. To this day, I still do not know how much money my mother and father earn. I don't know what type of insurance coverage they have or how they have invested their money. What I've learned about these things has been on my own through trial and error and educating myself through various publications. I've learned some hard and costly lessons during my life simply because I didn't know what to do but more importantly I didn't know what questions to ask.

This is why I wrote *The Real Life 101 Handbook*. I wanted to help others understand the basics of living that aren't taught in school. Again, I am not a millionaire. I don't have any magic get rich quick scheme that is going to make your financial life a breeze. I'm just a regular guy who wants to make a small contribution to the world by providing you with a comprehensive guide to the basic information you will need to manage your life. I hope you find the information useful.

Chapter 1 - My Story

IF YOU'RE like most people, you have received or are receiving your education from the public school system. You spend 12 years of your life doing exactly what is *required* of you. School is much like an obstacle course. Your "job" while in school is to navigate the paths laid before you by your teachers and to provide the "right" answers when tested to demonstrate you have "learned" what you were taught. If the ability to regurgitate facts learned through memorization were all that was required in life, you would be all set! Unfortunately, upon completing high school and receiving a diploma you have not learned much that is useful in the "Real World." Sure you may understand grammar, punctuation, spelling, and even be able to solve the most complicated math problem. These skills will not help you determine whether the lease you're about to sign for your first apartment needs to be modified. You have got to be able to *think on your own* to do that and you are not taught how to think for yourself in school.

Don't believe me? Well consider this - have you ever disagreed with a teacher in class? What was the result? I'm not talking about debating whether the answer to a math problem is 42 or 67. I mean disagreeing with a fundamental principle of economics or history or some other "truth" given to you by your teacher that you were being asked to willingly assimilate into your knowledge base as just that – unquestionable truth. Perhaps you were discussing Social Security or

Medicare and whether or not they are necessary in our society. What was the outcome? Was your teacher willing to listen to a contrary point of view? How about your classmates? If so, consider yourself lucky to have been exposed to someone who would force you to think on your own. What's more interesting to consider is how did your classmates respond? Did they support the debate or did they shun you for not agreeing with the teacher or just want you to shut up so the class could just keep going and you could get that lesson done?

The main purpose of school today is to teach conformity. Beginning with kindergarten you are taught how to follow rules, to do what you're told and what is expected of you. This philosophy is reinforced with each passing year as you progress through school. Your homework must be turned in at the specified time. You must answer the questions the way you were taught. Nonconformance is not acceptable. Conformance is rewarded and praised.

This is exactly what happened with me. I attended a parochial school from 1st thru 8th grade. I wore a uniform every day. I had homework to do. There was a lot expected from me. I was a B and C student. I was also with the same 20 to 30 kids for those 8 years and although we all became good friends the experience limited my view of the world. It was a very controlling atmosphere and absolute compliance was demanded. Nevertheless, there was comfort for me since I knew almost everyone in the school. Because the highest grade at the parochial school was 9th grade and my local high school was structured for 9th through 12th grade, I began attending public high school in the 9th grade.

The situation in public school was much different. First the school was much larger (I went from a school of 250 in 8th grade to a school of over 2,000 in 9th grade) which meant less one-on-one contact with the teachers. Nevertheless, when I had questions, I sought out the teachers and they were very willing to help me learn what I "needed" to learn. In 1988, I graduated high school 5th in my class of 580 with a 4.07 grade point average. Achieving all this you would think I was ready for the world but not just yet; I had been accepted to college.

I attended Georgia Tech and majored in Electrical Engineering. I spent the next 5 years of my life working to achieve my degree (5 years because I was part of the co-op program so I worked while I went to school). Georgia Tech is a fantastic school. People who were committed to learning and being the best they could be in their chosen field surrounded me. The environment pushed me to do more than I thought I could and it taught me a valuable lesson; if you want to succeed, you must surround yourself with the best. No average person will ever push you to do more than you believe is possible.

I also discovered that there is a big change from grade school to college. The guiding philosophy in college is somewhat different than that of the grade schools. Going to college teaches you how to solve problems when you do not have all the information available. They teach you how to seek out the information, where to find it and how to manipulate it to solve the problem. Although the primary focus is to teach you how to think, oftentimes you are still only taught *what* to think. When you take the test, there is still only one correct answer to each problem especially in an engineering curriculum.

The only class that really got me to think "out of the box" was a philosophy course I took to meet and ethics requirement necessary for graduation. Again, due to the "training" I received in grade school, I approached college the only way I had been taught – follow these rules, meet these requirements and do these things and you will be successful (i.e. get your degree). In all fairness to them, I might have gotten much more out of my college experience had I not approached my time there in that fashion. In all fairness to me, no one there guided me to approach things any differently than I already had.

What was the most enlightening to me was the exposure I received on my co-op job. I learned so much more than what I was taught in school. I had my first experiences with politics in the workplace. I realized that most of what I learned in college was theoretical and that "real world applications" were completely different. I was exposed to technology that was not part of my curriculum. In retrospect, the college did realize its shortcomings otherwise the co-op program would not have existed. But I had not had anyone challenge me to think for myself. So I graduated in June of 1993 with a 3.3 GPA and high honors (Cum Laude by most college standards). Sixteen years in school and the most critical life information had not been discussed and yet I thought I was ready to take on the world.

Yet, after all that education and all those years, no one had taught me how to buy a car, a house, or invest any money.

To my parent's credit, they did provide me with some basic tools. I had had a checking/savings account since I was about 12 years old where I had deposited birthday money, money from high school jobs and my co-op job. They had also co-singed for a Visa card for me to use during school. Unbeknown to me, these tools were helping me build a credit rating during my time in college. I only used the Visa card for large purchases and always made sure I would have money to pay the bill when it came due *before* I purchased anything. I wrote checks and balanced my checkbook each month. With this limited knowledge, I thought I was prepared to manage my life. I had plans to attend graduate school to obtain an advanced degree in Engineering Management. Everything was looking great...or so it seemed.

About 30 days before graduation I received a letter from the graduate school I had applied to indicating my application had been denied. I called the Dean of the School and learned that I did not have adequate work experience to be accepted into their program. I argued that my co-op job met the requirement but to no avail. So, after missing most of the on campus recruiting that had occurred 6 months earlier (that's right, companies come to campus to recruit in January for normal summer graduates), I began looking for my first "real" job.

In the summer of 1993, the US Economy was experiencing a recession. I interviewed for 3 months with almost 24 companies before I received an offer of employment. During that time, I lived with my parents and worked as a waiter to make money. I saved every dime to be ready to move out into the world. When the job finally came, I was ready to move on with my life.

Sometime during those 3 months, I received a phone call from my college roommate, David Emmerich. We had met our freshman year at Georgia Tech when we lived on the same residence hall. We soon became good friends and roomed together from our sophomore year until graduation. He too was in the co-op program so we had shared many similar experiences. After graduation, he had found a job and now lived in a different state. He said something to me on the phone that day that is the most poignant summation of my college experience: "Mike, I have discovered that I have a lot of knowledge but very little understanding." There was more wisdom in that statement than I think either of us realized.

After I accepted my job offer, I found an apartment near my new job, rented a moving truck and moved into my first place that was all my own. Then, I decided to reward myself for my new life with my first major purchase – a new stereo system. I ordered the components with my trusty credit card; total bill $2,000. I paid for it all when the bill was due just as I always had. Things were going really well and then I made my first big mistake – I bought a new car.

Buying the car was the first financial mistake I made in my life. I'll get into the details in a later chapter but for now the point is I was not prepared. I didn't have enough information to make a good decision or for that matter negotiate effectively. Why? No one had ever explained it to me. Not my parents, not anyone in school; no one. Now, I must share the blame because I didn't ask for any help. I'm sure if I had had the presence of mind to call my dad and talk to him, he would have helped me and provided the guidance I needed. But I had a college degree. I should be able to handle this, right? Well that wasn't the case as you read later. It comes down to this simple statement – You just don't know what you don't know.

The next 18 months after the car purchase brought tremendous change in my life. I changed jobs to do something more in line with my career goals. I met a girl, got married and now, with 3 years of "real" work experience under my belt, I applied to graduate school (this time for an MBA) at Arizona State University and was accepted. My wife and I relocated from South Carolina to Arizona and started a new adventure. During that time, I saved a lot of money in preparation for graduation, buying a house, starting a family, etc. I worked part time while going to school full time. I was careful to pay off our credit cards each month. As graduation approached, I received offers from 5 different companies. After much deliberation I accepted the job with a company in Connecticut. I relocated again and I purchased my first house but I almost lost it simply because, again, I didn't understand what was required. I had earned a graduate degree and spent 19 years undergoing formal education and no one had taught me how to buy a house! I'll tell you the whole story in Chapter 10 about buying a home.

After being in Connecticut for 3 months, I learned that another firm was purchasing my company and I would be laid-off. I began looking for work...again. Those were stressful times. We did have money saved and I was given a severance package but my life was put on hold. We really had to be careful how we spent our money because we didn't know how long I would be out of work. Thankfully, I had learned a lot about how to conduct a proper job search through the placement office of the MBA program at Arizona State University. The school did an exceptional job preparing us for our job search (we had our first class on the subject the first week of the 2 year program). After 5 months of searching, I found a new job which required yet another relocation. I also sold my first house and gained more experience.

The next 3 years in Virginia brought about more life changes. I bought another house and my 2nd new car. My wife and I had developed a net worth of over $100,000. Soon my wife became pregnant and we had a baby. Things seemed to be going very well but oftentimes that is exactly when life throws you the curve ball. Problems in my marriage that had been in the background for some time began to bubble to the surface. My wife and I separated and eventually divorced. I spent a lot of money on a lawyer. I had to sell my house and move into an apartment. I had to pay alimony and child support. I was fired from my job. Most of my net worth was wiped out. There were certainly no classes in school to prepare me for those challenges. It was an extremely difficult time for me. There were days when I thought I would never get my career or my life back on track. I received a lot of support from my family and eventually things began to turn around.

After 4 months, I did find another job. I began dating a woman and eventually bought another house. Again, things were going well but my new job was not working out as I expected so I began yet another job search and found a position that required yet another relocation. I sold and bought houses again. A few months after moving, I married my 2nd wife and her son came to live with us. We had our ups and downs together and I really thought things were beginning to work out for me. However almost 4 years later to the day my wife made an announcement nonchalantly that she wanted a divorce.

In case you've lost track, in the 15 years since I obtained my undergraduate degree, I have lived in 4 states, bought 4 houses and sold 3, worked for 7 different companies (8 if you count my co-op job in undergraduate school), gotten married, gotten a graduate degree, had a child, gotten divorced, gotten married a second time and gotten divorced again.

If you think I planned my life this way, you are nuts! Life doesn't always go the way you plan. The only way you can survive what comes your way is if you have prepared. That's why I wrote this book. I can't tell you everything you're going to need to know. Everyone's situation is different. Everyone has different needs. The purpose of this book is to give you the basic understanding you need to cope with the life situations you will encounter.

Thomas Edison once said, "Good fortune is what happens when opportunity meets with preparation." I hope the information contained in this book gives you the preparation you need to make your life successful regardless of what happens.

Chapter 2 - What to Do After High School

SO, AFTER spending 12 years of your life preparing, you're finally ready for the "real world". The whole world is out there for you and you can be whatever you want and do whatever you want to do (so long as it's not illegal). You can make your life whatever you want it to be. Now, how do you get started? Hopefully, you have already decided whether to attend college or go straight into the workforce. But, just in case, here are a few things for you to consider.

Each year, everything gets a little more expensive. Prices for everything from cars to groceries increase. This is commonly referred to as *inflation*. The federal government, through the Bureau of Labor and Statistics (BLS) measures price changes over time through something called the Consumer Price Index. This index tracks "changes in prices of all goods and services purchased for consumption by urban households. User fees (such as water and sewer service) and sales and excise taxes paid by the consumer are also included. Income taxes and investment items (like stocks, bonds, and life insurance) are not included." (Source www.bls.gov). The following chart illustrates the changes in the CPI from 1960 through 2007:

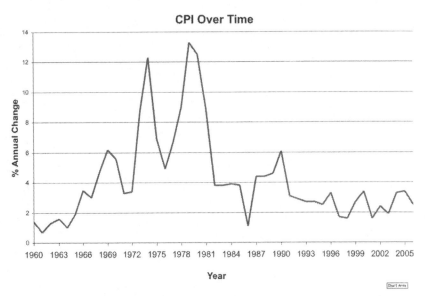

What does this mean? It means that every year since 1960 prices for everything have increased by some amount. Look at the graph carefully. The line represents the *actual change* in prices each year. Obviously prices increased at a faster rate during the periods from 1973-1974 and 1976-1980. These circumstances are defined by economists as periods of inflation. You can also see that for the last 10-15 years, the amount of annual increase has been declining, however, there still has been an increase each and every year.

As an example, in 1960, the average home cost $58,600. By the year 2000, the average had jumped to $119,600 (Source – US Census). Under these conditions if you work for minimum wage, you will find it difficult to pay your bills and still have money left over to enjoy life. Therefore, you need to carefully consider what you want to do for a career. You should of course choose something that you will enjoy doing but you also need to consider how much money you need to earn to have the lifestyle you want. As you may have learned in economics class, life is all about tradeoffs. You may find an absolute perfect job yet not be able to pay your bills. You also cannot work for long in a job that you hate even though it pays you extremely well. So you need to choose wisely.

Increasingly, a college degree is required to obtain a well paying job. What most folks don't tell you is that the college degree's main purpose is to get you your first job. After that, it's mainly your experience and accomplishments that get you hired or promoted. That has certainly been the case for me with the various employers I have had over the years. Even if you do not go to college, any training you have after high school only improves your chances of obtaining a well paying job. There are folks who have become multi millionaires without any formal education but these are rare occurrences. For most of us, the way we build our financial futures is through advanced education, hard work, the acquisition of assets (things that you own that pay *you* money like stock, bonds, rental property) and networking with others.

If you choose not to go to college, it doesn't mean you will not ever reach your financial dreams. It may take you a little longer to get there. You might decide to start your own business. Again, you can do whatever you want to do; just be aware that every job doesn't pay the same and the more you know and more credentials you possess, the better chance you have to get the job and the pay you desire.

You also have to consider how you will provide for others in your life. Do you want a large family? How will you support them? Will you and your spouse both work or will one stay home with the kids? How can you afford all you want for your life?

With the divorce rate at almost 50% in this country, men and women both need to have skills they can use to make their own livings. You may find the perfect mate and each of you working full time provides more than enough income for your lifestyle. That was certainly the case for me and my first wife; we were able to save a lot when we were both working. However, what if one of you is laid off, becomes ill or disabled. Will your lifestyle suffer as well? What if you mate decides to leave you after 5 years of marriage? Will you be able to support yourself and/or your children? Answering these questions now will help you choose the career that's best suited for your financial requirements. Remember, life doesn't always go as planned so you have to prepare.

What's the big deal anyway? Is it really that expensive for me to live on my own? I mean it's just me? Here are some numbers for some typical expenses in the average single person household:

Monthly Expense For:		Amount
Place to Live	$	*630.00*
Food	$	*250.00*
Auto Loan	$	*273.27*
Utilities (Electric, Water, Natural Gas)	$	*125.87*
Telephone	$	*40.24*
Cable TV/Satellite	$	*45.99*
Insurance (Auto)	$	*50.18*
Insurance (Property)	$	*20.34*
Gasoline	$	*100.00*
Total	$	*1,535.89*
Annualized Net Income (BEFORE Taxes)	$	*24,574.24*
Effective Hourly Pay Rate	$	*12.29*

As you can see, even making $12.29 an hour (over twice the 2007 minimum wage of $5.85/hr) doesn't go very far. In this example, you are not saving any money for your retirement or those unexpected things that happen in life like the car breaking down or having to pay your medical deductible for a trip to the hospital. You are not going out to eat, going on vacation, buying new clothes, etc.

Now, you could get a roommate and share some of the living expenses and that would help. However, relying completely on someone else for your financial well-being is never a good idea. Your goal should be to support your chosen lifestyle completely through your own income. Then, if you have someone else helping with expenses, you have more money to save or use for other "discretionary" items that can make life a bit more fun.

We will discuss expenses in more detail in Chapter 4 but first we need to obtain some income and for most folks, that means finding a job.

Chapter 3 - Getting a Job

WELL TO START earning money you first have to have a job. Depending upon your skills, abilities and education there are many different things you can do to earn money. You can work at the local Starbucks serving coffee. You could be a waiter or waitress at a Ruby Tuesdays. You might work in a manufacturing plant on 2nd shift (from 2pm to 10pm) making electrical assemblies. You might have a college education and work in a bank or in an engineering firm. There are many, many possibilities. So before we go much further with how to find a job, let's talk about how to decide what job is right for you.

There is a famous quote from Budda that reads "Find work that you love and you will never work a day in your life." That is so true. I have had jobs that I did not enjoy and it was an effort to get out of bed each day. The jobs I have liked were fun and easy to me. So think about what you like to do. Do you like to work with your hands? Do you like to do math? How about working with computers? Do you want to work with other people or alone?

That is quite a bit for you to consider but that is not the end. You also need to think about what type of education you will need to get the job you would like. If you want to be an electrical engineer that designs power control systems, you will most likely not get the job with only a high school degree and no experience. If you want to work serving coffee, you can probably get that job with just the high school diploma and little or no experience. The great thing about it; it is all up to you. You decide what you want to do and then you can determine what skills, education and experience you will need to acquire to reach your goal. Regardless of what you do, it is never too early to start getting experience by working.

My first paying job was working behind the counter in an auto parts store. I worked there during the summer months between my junior and senior year in high school. I learned a lot about cars that summer but I also learned how to manage inventory, interact with customers, keep things neat an organized and work with other people. Now, I wasn't ready to be CEO of a company after working there one summer but I had some experience. That is something an employer wants to see. What experience do you have that is going contribute to the success of the company? What makes you the right person for the job? But before you can answer an employer's questions, you have to get an interview. So, let's talk about how to get started finding your first job.

GETTING ORGANIZED

Before we start looking for a job, we need to get organized. The first step is to get a new notebook to use for your job search activity that we will call the Job Search Notebook (JSN). Divide your notebook into these sections:

1. *Identify Potential Jobs* – You will use this part of your JSN to keep track of the jobs that interest you and the activities you have taken towards obtaining the job;

2. *About Me* – In this section, list everything about you such as your education, activities you have done at school, sports you play, awards you have won, accomplishments, things you like to do, talents and skills you have, etc. Try to answer the questions "What makes you who you are and what do you do when you are not in school?";

3. *Interviewing* – Keep all your basic information about interviewing in this section including your interviewing script, your interview questions and answers;

Now we need to collect some information to insure you get that job!

IDENIFY POTENTIAL JOBS

You want a job to earn money. Companies need workers to make their firms successful. So how do you find out who is hiring? There are several sources you can use to find jobs: the newspaper, internet job boards (Monster, Careerbuilder, etc), temporary employment agencies, the local job service (a state government agency) and simply asking. Each of these resources will help you find jobs in your area that employers are trying to fill. I am not trying to tell you everything about finding a job in this book since there are thousands of books and internet resources on the subject. However, I will present a simple example of how to find a summer job to earn some money while you're still in high school. There are three ways to find this type of job: the classifieds in the newspaper, the local job service and just asking.

First, we'll use the newspaper method. Buy a copy of your local Sunday paper and look through the classifieds for job opening. It is very important to get the Sunday paper because the most jobs are advertised in the Sunday edition. Another option is to go the website of your local newspaper and look through their classifieds section on-line. Now you need your JSN. Scan through and make notes about the jobs that interest you such as the name of the job, the date that you noticed the advertisement, a brief description of the job and the phone number listed in the advertisement. You may even want to include a copy of the job advertisement. Use a separate page for each job and make notes including dates you have any "activity" about that job such as calling to request an interview.

Another source is your local job service. Each state has a department that collects information about job openings from employers in your area. You can use any search engine to find this information by typing in your state's name and the word "government" such as "South Carolina Government." Then look around the site for headings including the word "employment." You will find many resources that will help you identify jobs that are available in your area.

Before you discuss a job with an employer, you want to do some research about how much money you can expect to earn from the job. Many job advertisements indicate the pay rate for the job but sometimes you will not find out until the interview. Sometimes the amount you are paid for the job is negotiable and other times you will be told what the job pays and there is no negotiation. Either way you need to be sure the amount of pay is reasonable for the job you are seeking. How do you find out what is reasonable?

There is a book called the Occupational Outlook Handbook (OOH) that is published by the United States Government. When I first used it, the internet did not yet exist and I had to go to the library to look at it and it was one of those books they would not let you check out. But now, you no longer have to go to the library because it is available on-line through the United States Government Bureau of Labor and Statistics (BLS) at *www.bls.gov/oco*. You can search through it to find information on just about any occupation. I typed in "coffee" in the search box and with a few mouse clicks I know that the average hourly wage for coffee service worker is about $8.15. The OOH is updated every two years so the information is fairly accurate. You can use it to help you evaluate what a job is worth. For example, if you were offered $8.79 per hour to work in a coffee shop, you would know you were getting a fair wage for the work. If you were offered $5.25, you might ask why the wage is so far below the national average for that type of work.

ABOUT ME

This next section of your JSN will be help you begin to develop a resume. A resume is a document that you can send to an employer to tell them a little bit about your education, qualifications and your abilities. For a part time job during high school you will probably not need one but it is good to start developing the information you need so that you will have it handy to develop your resume when it is needed. I'm not going to go into a lot of details about developing a resume here since there are many books and resources on the internet that can help you. If you type "Resume Help" in any search engine you will find many sources of information. This file (www.bls.gov/opub/ooq/1999/summer/art01.pdf) from the OOH website explains how to develop a resume. This site (www.resume-help.org/) also has some good basic information. Make sure you create your resume in Microsoft Word® as this is the standard used by most employers for electronic resumes.

You should also develop a list of references and take it with you to your interview. References are people who can verify your qualifications to an employer. Be sure to include the person's name, address, phone number and email address. Choose people who will speak highly of you and avoid using relatives as references. Last but not least get permission from these people before listing them on your application. You will find that most people will be more than happy to help you.

INTERVIEWING

Before you identify a few jobs that interest you, you will need to prepare yourself for the job interview. We will break this process into several steps:

1. Preparing for the interview;
2. Asking for an interview;
3. Conducting the interview;
4. Following up after the interview;

Preparing for the interview – Look over the information you prepared in the About Me section of your JSN about your skills and experience for the interview. Ask yourself what have you done in school that demonstrates your skills and abilities? Were you in any clubs? Were you a leader in the club or in another group? Have you volunteered with your church or some other organization? Were you in Cub Scouts, Boy Scouts or Girl Scouts? What about any team sports? Did you play basketball, football or soccer? In each of these activities, you learned skills and grew as a person. When an employer asks you "What experience do you have working with other people?" you can respond:

> *"I have been on the basketball team for the last 2 years. Being part of that team has taught me how working together creates success and that failure is everyone's responsibility. We always win as a team and lose as a team. My teamwork skills will help me contribute to the success of your organization."*

See how that works? You may not have "work" experience but you have plenty of experiences that have helped prepare you for a job. One thing you know about is homework so be sure to do yours for your job interview! Look over the requirements in the job advertisement. When you call to ask for the interview, see what else you can learn about the job. What will you be doing? Working with a team or alone? Working outside or inside? Will you be speaking directly to customers? Then sit down and make some notes in your job search notebook about what is needed to do the job and what experience you have that meets those needs. It can be a very simple list:

Job Requirements	*My Abilities*
Teamwork Skills	*2 Years Basketball Team*
Reliable	*No Tardies at School for 4 years*
Organized	*Pocket Calendar to Keep Appointments*
Hard Working	*Extra Practice to Learn New Basketball Plays*

You get the idea. Just sit down somewhere quiet and think about it and you will be amazed how many things come to mind. Use your JSN to develop these lists. You should also write down some responses to some of the most popular questions asked during interviews:

1. *Tell me about yourself* – You want your response to this question to focus on who you are such as "I am a self motivated, hard working person who likes to complete challenging tasks. I enjoy working with people and being part of a winning team." Again, think about who you are and use your JSN to develop your answers;

2. *What are your strengths and weaknesses?* Add this list to your JSN. Here is a secret: Every weakness you have is simply an overdone strength. That's hard to believe but it is true! I learned this at a seminar that was given by Dusty Staub who is a very well respected leadership consultant (www.staubleadership. com/). Think about what do you do very well and what you do not so well and you will see. For example, if you have an incredible ability to concentrate and get a job done, that is a great strength. If you are too focused, you can miss important details because you are too focused on getting the task done. Work on your list of strengths, get feedback from others about your list and make sure you can discuss your strengths and weaknesses in detail comfortably;

3. *Why should we hire you?* This is a great question and one that you can easily answer after you have done your homework about the job and know what skills you have that are applicable. Just tell them the skills you have that meet their needs;

24

4. *Tell me about a time when...* You may receive several questions like this that are called Behavioral Interview Questions. With these types of questions, the employer will try to learn more about how you handle situations that are presented to you. For example, "Tell me about a time when you had to deal with a difficult person." You might tell your employer about someone who was on your basketball team that was not playing well with the team and how you helped them become more of a team player. Or you might discuss a time you helped settle an argument between two of your friends. The specific example is not as important as WHAT you did in the situation.

Practice, practice, and practice again your responses. Only if you have prepared well will you present yourself as a confident applicant for the job.

Asking for the interview - In your job search notebook, develop an "interview script" that you can use to ask for an interview. It might look something like this:

> *"Hello. My name is _____ and I am calling about the position you advertised in the (Name of Newspaper) for a (Name of job). I would like to meet with you to discuss the job in more detail. When will you be conducting interviews?"*

Practice your script so it does not sound like you are reading from it when you are on the phone. Have someone you trust review your script and let them give you some suggestions about how you might improve it. During your first phone call with the employer, they may ask you a few questions about your experience, etc. How do you answer these questions since this is you first job interview and you do not have any experience? It is actually pretty easy because you have a lot more experience than you think.

Conducting the Interview – Now that you have an interview scheduled, you need to prepare for the interview itself. When you attend the interview, you will most likely have to fill out an application form. You will also need to provide information to the employer such as your full name, date of birth, Social Security Number, Address, work history and education. You may need to bring these items to the interview:

- Social Security Card;
- Government-Issued Identification (e.g. driver's license, passport);
- Resume or completed application;
- References;
- Transcripts from your school

The best way to be prepared is to ask the employer what information they will need from you BEFORE you go to the interview. When you arrive for the interview you will have a brief meeting with someone from the company who will ask you questions to get to know you better and understand better your skills and qualifications. Here are some other things to consider from the Occupational Outlook Handbook website for the interview:

- Be well groomed;
- Dress appropriately;
- Do not chew gum or smoke;
- Be early;
- Learn the name of your interviewer and greet him or her with a firm handshake;
- Use good manners with everyone you meet;
- Relax and answer each question concisely and professionally;
- Use proper English—avoid slang;
- Be cooperative and enthusiastic;
- Use body language to show interest—use eye contact and don't slouch;
- Ask questions about the position and the organization, but avoid questions whose answers can easily be found on the company Web site;

When the interview is concluding, thank the interviewer for his or her time and tell them that you would like to have the job. Ask them when you can expect to hear from them. Be sure to get a business card from them, thank them again and shake his or her hand firmly but not too strongly.

One word of caution – do not discuss money with the employer in the beginning. Well, aren't we looking for a job to get some money? That is true but think about it this way; if you wanted someone to clean up your room for you and the first thing they asked was "How much are you going to pay me?" what really interests them? Do they want to clean your room or are they just looking for money? Exactly. Although money is an important consideration, you want to be sure the employer realizes that you are most interested in the job. You can discuss money later when they offer you the job!

Following Up After the Interview: When you get home, send a note by mail or an email to the interviewer thanking them again for their time and consideration. Emphasize anything you can remember from the interview that indicated you were a good fit for the position such as "I am confident that my teamwork skills with contribute to the great team you have built at your organization." If you have not heard anything by the time they promised, call them and follow up.

When they offer you the job, make sure you understand the pay rate. If it does not match with the information you obtained from the OOH <u>and</u> you think it is too low, you can call and discuss it with them. Explain to them that you had researched the pay rate in the OOH and you wanted to understand why their offer did not agree with the information you collected. If they do not change their offer, you have to decide if their reasons are reasonable. If you decide to accept the job, thank them for the opportunity and congratulations – you are ready to start earning some money!

FINAL THOUGHTS

This chapter is intended to serve as an introduction on how to find a job. There are so many other things we need to cover in this book that there is simply not enough space to explain everything you need to know about finding a job. There are many resources that you can use from books to the internet to guidance counselors to consultants that can help you learn more about the job search process so make good use of them.

This is also a good place to remind you that this book is not intended to answer every question about the topics I cover. If you do not get anything else out of this book please remember this – <u>you must learn to think for yourself</u>. I will provide you with some basic information to get you started but you must take the initiative to seek out additional resources and learn as much as you can about these topics. Knowledge is power and the only way you will obtain it is to seek it out on your own. If you will always do that, you will find the information you need to make the best decisions for you and your life.

Now, we've started earning some money and before we lose it all we need to learn how to manage it!

Chapter 4 - Managing Your Cash Flow

WE DISCUSSED Cash Flow a little bit in Chapter 2. Cash Flow is simply the amount of money you have left over after you have paid all your expenses. This is the single most important number in your financial life. The best part is it is completely up to you! How you choose to spend your money determines how much you have left over each month. In Chapter 3, we discussed how to find a job so now we need to talk about how you will be paid for your work and what your paycheck will look like.

THE PAYCHECK

Regardless of whether you work for a small private company like Bob's Auto Repair or a large multination corporation like General Electric, you will receive a regular paycheck. This paycheck will be based upon two compensation methods:

1. Hourly Wages / No College Degree – In an hourly (also called "Blue Collar") job, you will earn money based upon the number of hours you work each week. Generally, you are paid a certain wage rate called Straight Time for each hour worked during the week up to 40 hours. After 40 hours, you are paid Overtime and *generally* this is at the rate of 1.5 times your Straight Time rate.

2. <u>Salary Wages / College Degree</u> – In a salary (also called "White Collar") job, you are paid the same amount each week *regardless* of the number of hours you work. Do not get too excited; the employer has an expectation that you will work a minimum of 40 hours per week. The difference is you will *not* receive overtime for any time worked over 40 hours. In most cases, if you calculate the equivalent hourly pay for a salary job, it is a little higher than you would receive for straight hourly work. There are also some situations where you can receive a salary *and* overtime but these are becoming more rare.

These are guidelines and not rules. There are people without college degrees who are paid a salary and vice versa. Each situation is unique but this gives you some basic understanding of compensation.

DEDUCTIONS

So once you have a job and are receiving a paycheck you are all set, right? Almost. First we need to talk about what your paycheck will look like. Before you have reached an agreement with your employer about the amount of money you will be paid, you need to understand that you will not receive that exact amount in your paycheck. There are several deductions that occur on your paycheck. A *deduction* is any amount that is taken away from your compensation before you receive your paycheck. So, when you negotiate a salary or hourly wage rate with your employer, you are determining the amount of *Gross Pay* you will receive which is the amount of money you make before any deductions are taken from your check. The deductions are then taken from that Gross Pay to arrive at your *Net Pay* or the amount of money you receive in your check also called *Take Home Pay.* There are 2 main categories of these deductions – Taxes and Benefits. Taxes include Federal Income Tax, State Income Tax (which varies by state), Social Security, and Medicare. These will be deducted from each paycheck you receive and there is nothing you can do about it. The government just takes this money. Benefits include Health Insurance Costs (which we will discuss in more detail in Chapter 8) and any other deductions you decide to include (such as contributions to a 401k discussed in

Chapter 11).

Now we can review an example to show you what the paycheck would look like. In this example, we will assume that you have gotten your first job, have negotiated a salary of $30,000 per year with no overtime, you are paid 24 times per year (every two weeks or bi-weekly) and you are not going to save any money in a 401k.

My First Job Assumptions	Amount
Annual GROSS Salary (Note 1)	$ 30,000.00
Bi-Weekly GROSS Pay	$ 1,250.00
TAXES (Annual Amounts)	
Federal Income Tax (Note 2)	$ 4,237.50
State Income Tax (Note 3)	$ 1,742.00
Federal Medicare 1.45%	$ 435.00
Federal Social Security 6.2% (Note 4)	$ 1,860.00
Total Annual Taxes	$ 8,274.50
Total Bi-Weekly Taxes	$ 344.77
Effective Tax Rate – ALL Taxes	27.58%
BENEFITS	
Annual Medical Insurance (Note 5)	$ 559.00
Bi Weekly Medical	$ 23.29
Total Bi-Weekly Deductions	$ 368.06
Bi-Weekly NET Income	$ 881.94
Monthly NET Income	$ 1,763.88
Annualized Net Income	$ 21,166.56
% of Pay Retained (NET/GROSS)	70.56%
Effective GROSS Hourly Pay Rate	$ 15.00

Notes:
1. Average, single person income in 2002 (last data available from the Census Bureau) was $25,406. Adjusted to $30,000 for use in this example.
2. Federal Income Tax in 2004 for $30,000 annual income is $4,000 plus 25% of the amount over $29,050 for a total of $4,237.50
3. For this example, we will use South Carolina's tax from the 2004 SC Tax Table.
4. For 2004, the Social Security tax rate is 6.20% and the Medicare tax rate is 1.45%.
5. Annual medical expenses were $508 for single person coverage in 2003 according to a survey conducted by Kaiser Family Foundation and Heath Research Educational Trust. Assume a 10% increase for 2004 to $559 per year

As you can see from the example, to make a $30,000 salary you would need to find an hourly job that paid almost 3 times the Federal Minimum Wage of $5.15 per hour! Also, you have discovered the first reality of personal finance – the government takes a healthy portion of your money each year. In this example you are paying almost $8,300 or 28% of your income in taxes to both the federal and state government *every year*. This does *not* include the money you will pay in sales taxes each time you purchase anything nor does it include any property taxes you may owe on vehicles you own (if your state has vehicle property taxes). In other words, making $2,500 in Gross pay each month, you will work from January to April 20th (3.3 months) each year just to pay your income taxes! In fact many organizations estimate that the actual tax rate for all taxes paid by individuals is approaching 50% of their income. Keep this in mind when you hear politicians claim that tax rates are low and no additional tax cuts are needed.

BASIC EXPENSES

Since we have developed the true picture of what you will earn each month, let's plug that into our expense example from Chapter 2:

Monthly Cash Flow Statement:	Amount
INCOME	
Total NET Monthly Income	*$ 1,763.88*
EXPENSES	
Place to Live (Apartment Rent)	*$ 630.00*
Food	*$ 250.00*
Auto Loan	*$ 273.27*
Utilities (Electric, Water, Natural Gas)	*$ 125.87*
Telephone	*$ 40.24*
Cable TV/Satellite	*$ 45.99*
Insurance (Auto)	*$ 50.18*
Insurance (Property)	*$ 20.34*
Gasoline	*$ 100.00*
Property Taxes on Car (Estimate based on SC Rates)	*$ 37.50*
Total Expenses	*$ 1,573.39*
Amount Remaining	*$ 190.49*
% EXPENSES as a percent of INCOME	*89.20%*

This is an extremely simplified example of a Cash Flow statement. Actually it is an *Income Statement* as an accountant would define it. However, at this point, we are assuming that all bills are paid immediately when you receive them so the Cash Flow Statement and Income Statements would be identical. We will get into some more detail about these financial status reports in Chapter 6.

So, what do you think of your financial position? Is $30,000 per year enough money? What will you do with the extra $190 you have each month? Remember, this example does not have any expenses for going out to eat, attending concerts, buying music, or buying gifts for birthdays or Christmas. It also does not include monies needed for any unexpected expenses such as car repairs or hospital bills (that's right, even though you are paying for medical insurance, you will still have some money you will have to pay if you get sick called *Out-of-Pocket expenses*). Also, you are not saving any money for retirement. Going along like this could create some severe financial problems for you down the road when the unexpected happens and it will – believe me.

DEVELOPING A FINANCIAL PLAN

The main goal in your financial plan is to conserve cash. Pay bills on time but pay them when they are due not earlier. Stretch your money as far as you can and establish a good bill payment schedule so that your income and expenses are flowing at the same rate. For example, on the Cash Flow Statement example, your net income is $1,763.88 each month but you are paid half that every two weeks. You do not want all your bills to be due on the first of the month or you will always have problems keeping up. Work with your "suppliers" (electricity company, phone company, gas company, auto loan company, etc.) to establish different payment dates for each bill. Most companies will provide you with several payment date options. Establish the bill pay dates so they match well with your income flow.

You can also set up your bills to be automatically drafted from your bank account or charged to your credit card each month but be careful that you always have enough money in your accounts to cover these automatic transactions. In the movie *Contact* with Jodie Foster, there is one scene where she is getting ready to get into the "machine" they had built that will supposedly transport her to another world. A man hands her a cyanide pill and explains that "there are 1,000 reasons why you may need to take this; it's the reasons we can't think of that make it necessary." The point is you will always need extra cash on hand for the things you cannot anticipate. But what could happen?

What would you do if you lost your job? You could be fired because you boss has decided he just does not like you. You might say "They can't do that" but they can and they will. There are a multitude of reasons you could lose your job through no fault of your own. Unless you are willing to hire an attorney who charges you $200 per hour and wait a few years for your case to go through court, you will not have much recourse after being fired. I am not saying that you should not fight for your rights. There are many situations where folks have done so and won when the employer terminated them without cause or discriminated against them in some way. However, these situations are hard to prove and take lots of time and money to pursue which is difficult to do when you are unemployed. You may be eligible for unemployment but the amount of money in your unemployment check might only be 50% of your previous gross income. As if that was not enough of a blow to your finances, the government still taxes your unemployment check as income!

How can we improve the situation? There are only two ways – make more money or spend less each month. Both of these are completely in your control although once you have a job it is not easy to increase your income whenever you wish. You might decide to look for another job that will pay more. However, that may not be possible based upon the area in which you live, how the overall economy is performing, etc. You could spend some time with your current employer demonstrating your capabilities and work towards a promotion however it might take 2-3 years before the promotion is available. The most immediate thing you can do is to reduce your expenses.

Is the $650 per month apartment really worth it? Could you live somewhere else that was less expensive? Also, could you find some roommates to share the cost keeping in mind there is a risk of relying on someone else for your financial security? How important is it to you to have all the cable or satellite channels at your disposal? Would basic cable at $9.95 per month be acceptable? Could you find another car that would meet your needs but be less expensive to operate? If your find an older car that meets your needs, the property taxes you pay would also most likely be reduced. Unfortunately, owning an older car may require you to save more in case you have to pay for repairs. Perhaps you do not need a car at all and can ride the subway or bus or a bicycle to work?

You should keep all these things in mind before you accept your first job. Make sure you negotiate the highest salary that is reasonable for someone with your experience and qualifications. You only get once chance to establish your income during your job negotiation. Once the salary is set, it will be very difficult for you to increase it without some major life changes that could require you to relocate to another town or state. Also, you need to clearly understand your financial situation before you make any commitments to sign an apartment lease (Chapter 7), car or home loan (Chapters 9 & 10).

SAVINGS GOALS

Setting up a budget (Chapter 6) is the best way to insure you meet your financial goals. As part of establishing the budget, you should include a line item in your expenses to pay yourself first. This should take two forms – *Short Term* and *Long Term* savings. Short Term savings is money you can get your hands on quickly when the unexpected happens. Another term for this is Liquid Assets or Cash. This is the money you have in your checking or savings account that you can easily use to pay bills.

Long Term savings is money you invest to save for retirement or some time in the future. These *Non-Liquid Assets* can become *Liquid* assets but it takes some time. For example, if you need $2,500 to pay for a medical bill, you may have to sell some stock you own to have enough money to do it. Depending on the broker you use, it may take 5-7 *business* days for the cash to actually be available to you. So, as a general rule, you should have enough money in your Liquid Assets to cover 2 months worth of expenses and enough in your Non-Liquid Assets to cover another 4 months of expenses.

Another thing to keep in mind when the unexpected happens is that *everything is negotiable.* Most people do not understand this simple concept. Going back to the $2,500 medical bill, you may be able to work out an interest free payment plan with the medical provider so that you pay off that amount over a 6 month period. Having to only add an extra $417 per month to your budget rather than having to pay off the entire amount at once would give you time to reduce your discretionary spending (i.e. money you spend on whatever you want) and prevent you from having to sell some of your non-liquid assets. But look back at our example Cash Flow Statement. This means you would need to find another $225 a month to make this commitment. All the more reason you should have additional liquid assets in reserve.

The only time you might have more difficulty negotiating a payment plan is with government agencies and utilities since they usually want to be paid in full. However, it is still possible to negotiate with them. The key is to find the person in the organization that can make a decision for you. Not just the customer service representative you speak to on the phone but his/her boss, manager or someone at a higher level in the organization. Ideally you would want to meet with this individual in person and make your case for what you want to do but you may also be able to do it over the phone. Even if you do not get everything you want, if you get them to change the situation to your advantage in any way, you have gotten something.

This brings me to a very important point. Negotiation skills are very important in any aspect of your life. I highly recommend you read the book *Getting to Yes: Negotiating Agreement Without Giving In* by Roger Fisher, William Ury, and Bruce Patton. As they say in their introduction "Like it or not, you are a negotiator. Negotiation is a fact of life...Everyone negotiates something every day." You have to become comfortable asking for what you want and working towards your objectives. Do not assume that what has been set before you is all that is available.

All these decisions you have to evaluate to determine what is the best course of action for your unique situation. As I mentioned before, life is all about trade-offs. You have to evaluate all the different possibilities and decide how best to spend the limited resources (i.e. net income) you receive each month. It is totally your decision – no one else can decide but you what is best. It can be scary to have to determine all these things on your own and you <u>will</u> make mistakes. That is alright as many of life's lessons are best learned the hard way; most of my best lessons have happened to me that way. I wrote this book to give you some basic guidance so you can avoid some of the major mistakes I made. Now that we understand a little more about the beginnings of our new financial life, let's talk about how we manage that money at the Bank.

Chapter 5 - Money & Banking Basics

IF YOU'RE like most kids today, you have very little idea how a bank works. You have probably received money from your relatives for birthdays or at holidays and you might even receive an allowance. Generally you received these gifts in the forms of cash or a check. You probably keep your money in a "piggy bank" or some other container in your room and you grab some when you need it. Perhaps your parents have opened a savings account at the bank for you to keep your money in a safer place. Chances are you do not have your own checking account and have not started managing your money at the bank with any sophistication.

Did you ever wonder how a check you recieve gets turned into cash? What do you need to set up a checking account? What does it mean when you "establish credit?" Should you set up a savings account too? Why is the Government the only group that prints money? These and many other questions we will answer in this chapter.

HISTORY OF MONEY

Money or Currency has been around for such a long time that most folks forget that the original system used for obtaining goods and services was *Barter*. Barter is another word for trading. In the early history of civilization, most people were self-sufficient. They grew their own food, hunted and built anything they needed on their own. Rarely was more produced then was actually needed and with good reason. If these folks grew enough corn to feed their family and two others, what would they do with excess? They did not have a freezer to store it. It would also require a lot more work to produce that amount of corn than just the exact amount needed for the individual family. It made perfect sense but was not very efficient.

As tribes and communities formed, hunting and gathering became more efficient and groups began to specialize in certain areas. Some people were better farmers than hunters so they did the farming for the whole tribe. The same was true for the hunters. But, now there were "extra" items. The farmers produced too much food for the tribe. What should they do with it? This is how barter began. People from a different tribe may have had too many animal skins but not enough food. Therefore, the two tribes would trade and each tribe would get what they needed.

However, even though this system was improved it was still imperfect. How much food is an animal skin worth? What if the other tribe needed more hunting gear than food? The trade between the two tribes would not work. There needed to be a common means of valuation for all the goods and services. Money was the answer.

Think about this today. There are hundreds of multinational companies that make the products that you purchase. Does Apple Computer make automobiles? Does Toyota Motor Company make dishwashing soap? Of course not; these companies have specialized in unique products and services because it is more efficient and keeps the costs of everything lower than they would be otherwise. So how many boxes of dishwashing soap do you need to trade to get a new iMac? You don't need to worry about it because we use money to purchase these goods.

There are two main criteria for using money. First, it has to be portable. If we were using bowling balls as our currency we would all be very strong but purchasing anything would be difficult. Second, it has to be accepted by everyone. During the United States Civil War, several of the states developed their own currency called *script*. This worked fine for transactions made within the state but did not work well when doing business with other states. In 1863 the National Banking Act established a national currency that is manufactured by the Treasury Department of the US Government.

If you think about it, the US Currency (Dollars, Quarters, Dimes, Nickels and Pennies) meets both of the main criteria. There is one additional key aspect of *fiat currency* or money produced by the government. The intrinsic value of the money is much different than the value we as "traders" place upon it. For example, the intrinsic value of a one dollar bill (i.e. what the paper and ink is actually worth on its own) is the *same* as a thousand dollar bill. The cost to print the money is identical. What makes them worth different amounts is everyone's perception of what they are worth. Let's look at some of the features of the money we use.

First of all, reproductions like this of actual US currency are not allowed unless they are in black and white and are either 1.5 times larger or 0.75 smaller than actual size. Notice the words across the top "Federal Reserve Note" have replaced the words "Silver Certificate" which was used when all money was backed by a certain amount of precious metal (silver bullion) that was held by the Federal Reserve. Secondly, the words across the top "Federal Reserve Note" have replaced the words "Silver Certificate" which was used when all money was backed by a certain amount of precious metal (silver bullion) that was held by the Federal Reserve. Later, our dollars were linked to a Gold Standard with each dollar being worth an equivalent fixed amount of gold that was roughly $35/ounce of gold. This meant the US Government had to hold these precious metals to "back up" all the currency that was in circulation. One of the most famous places this gold was stored is Fort Knox. On August 15th, 1971, President Nixon abolished this system, called the Bretton Woods System, when he took the country off the Gold Standard. He did this because the value of the dollar could not change rapidly enough in response to market changes in supply and demand which lead to misinformation about the costs of goods and services.

CURRENCY VALUE

Today, the Federal Reserve (the Fed), controls the value of the dollar by controlling the Money Supply or the amount of currency in circulation. The Fed accomplishes this using two methods. First, the Fed buys government securities from banks in the United States. This gives the banks cash that they can use to issue loans or for other cash needs of their business. The law requires the bank set aside 10% of its cash in "reserve" so there is cash available if it is needed. Second, the Fed adjusts the *Discount Rate,* also called the *Federal Funds Rate*, which is the interest rate the Fed charges banks when they borrow money from the Fed. As the rate lowers, more money is put into circulation and it is easier for both individuals and businesses to borrow money from banks. The value of the currency is determined by simple supply and demand or, in other words, how many people are trying to "buy" dollars relative to how many dollars are available.

The system has another level of complexity since the dollar is traded with other countries for their currency to support international trade. For example, if you want to buy something from England, you must pay for it in their currency, *Pounds Sterling* or the universal European currency the *Euro*. For you to do this, you must trade your dollars for British Pounds or Euros. This affects the supply and demand for Dollars, Pounds and Euros and consequentially the value of each.

While most people still use cash for many of their transactions, other means of payment have developed that make the transactions even more efficient and secure. Again, money needs to be portable. If you have a $300 car payment due, do you want to walk around with all that cash in you pocket? In addition, you most likely need to send the payment to some place that is out of your state. Most companies will not accept cash in the mail and it's never a good idea to send cash that way. So how do you pay that bill? You need a checking account.

CHECKING AND SAVINGS ACCOUNTS

Checking and Savings accounts are the most fundamental financial accounts you will have. They are the building blocks for your financial future. A Checking Account allows you to write a check that performs the function of moving money from your bank account to whomever you issued the check. The Savings Account is a place to store your money until you need it. The bank will pay you a small amount each month called *interest* because you are allowing them to hold your money. The interest rate on both accounts will be low (usually less than 1-2% per year) with the checking account having a lower rate. Why? Because the money will be moving in and out of your checking account on a regular basis so the bank knows it will not get to "hold" the money very long.

You'll need between $50-$100 to open a checking account. There are many options for the types of accounts you can open and you should review carefully the information about the various accounts from your bank. You should look for an account that does not have any fees, allows unlimited check writing, and has an ATM card that is tied to the account so you can get cash anytime day or night. Make sure the ATM card is NOT a debit card but for ATM access only. That way, if it is lost or stolen, the thief cannot drain your money out of your account by charging things. Review the banks policy for what fees you will be charged if you use an ATM outside their network. In general, a bank will charge you $2-$3 per transaction for using an ATM at another bank. You can avoid this by finding a bank and has many locations throughout your geographic area so you will always be able to use one of their ATMs. You may also have to maintain a minimum balance in your account to get these features so be sure to plan for that in your budget. In fact, the minimum balance is a nice cushion for those unexpected expenses we discussed earlier.

Once you open the account, you will receive a checkbook with checks that look similar to this:

Each check includes the same critical information. In the top left corner is your name and address. Although not in this example, it is a good idea to include your 10-digit phone number as well. You do NOT want to put your Social Security or Driver's License number on the check to protect yourself against identity theft.

The bank name and address appears in the lower left corner. At the bottom of the check is a series of numbers. The 9-digit Bank Routing number insures the check gets back to your bank when it is "cashed". The account number lets your bank know that you wrote this check and the amount should come out of your account. Finally, the check number in the top right corner identifies this check as a unique transaction for your account.

So as an example, we will fill out a check for your car payment. Let's say you have bought a new Volkswagen Beetle and financed it through Volkswagen Credit. Your monthly payment is $273.27 and loan account number with Volkswagen is 8542127.

Here's what the check would look like:

First, you would write the date and then "Volkswagen Credit" in the "Pay to the Order Of Line". Next, you would fill in 273.27 after the $ sign and also write "Two Hundred Seventy Three and 27/100" in the space before the word "Dollars". You do this as a protection because the written number ("Two Hundred...") should match the actual numbers you placed in the box. Banks look to make sure that these match so someone could not turn your $273.27 into $2,732.70. Therefore you should always begin writing the numbers or written text far to the left and add the "----" lines after (see the example) to take up any extra space to help insure no one can change your check.

In the "Memo" section (sometimes labeled the "For" line) you should include your account number for the loan you have with Volkswagen. This insures Volkswagen applies this payment to your outstanding loan and not some else's. After you have written the check, you want to record it in your Check Register.

The *check register* (or Registry) is what you use to keep track of the amount of money in your checking account. You record each deposit (called a *credit*) and payment or withdrawal (called a *debit*) made to the account. For each check you write you include the check number, date, who you paid and the amount. You then subtract the amount from the balance of your checking account. Let's say you have a balance of $1,274 on February 26th and you have entered some recent transactions. Here's what the Registry would look like:

SAMPLE CHECK REGISTER

Number Code	Date	Transaction Description	Payment (Debit)	Deposit (Credit)	Balance
	2/28	Paycheck		1,763.88	3,3037.88
98	3/1	Open Arms Apartments	650		2,387.88
Auto	3/7	Be All Wireless Phone	40		2,347.88

99	3/9	Consolidate Electric Utilities	55.12		2,292.76
100	3/10	Kroger Foods (Groceries)	60.25		2,232.51
	3/12	Withdraw Cash from ATM	20		2,212.51
101	3/15	Volkswagen Credit	273.27		1,939.24

A word of caution. Do not get confused between the balance you have in your Registry and what the bank says you have in your account. For example, let's say you call the bank on 3/15 to ask how much money you have in your account and they tell you its $2,327.88. Looking at the sample check register, you think "Fantastic" because you believe you only have $1,939.24. Actually, your amount is correct and the bank is wrong. But how is that possible?

It happens because there is a time delay from when you write a check until it *clears* the bank or, in other words, before the bank takes money out of your account. Generally, it takes 7-10 business days for a check to clear. It takes so long because the check has to go through a process to be turned into cash. The person to whom you wrote the check takes the check to their bank to cash it or deposit it into their account. Their bank "advances" them money and then sends the check to your bank and requests that your bank reimburse them for the advance. Your bank processes your check, removes the funds from your account and sends it to the other person's bank.

So, on 3/15 the bank is NOT aware that you have written checks number 99, 100 and 101. They are aware of the ATM withdrawal you made on 3/12 since the ATM is linked into their computer system. So the balance of $2,347.88 in your register on 3/7 minus the ATM amount of $20 is all the bank "knows" you have taken out of your account. If you continue to write checks thinking you have $2,327.88 in your account when you actually have just over $1,900, you could wind up *overdrawing* your account (taking more money out than is available). This is commonly referred to as "bouncing a check" and is a bad situation for everyone, especially you. When this happens, most banks charge a fee to you or worse your check will not be honored. If your check is not honored, it is returned to the person to whom you issued the check and they may impose a fee. Doing this too often can have a negative affect on your credit report (which we will discuss later in this chapter).

So how do your insure that you and the bank know what is happening with your account? Each month, the bank will send you a statement showing all the activity for your checking account for that month. When you receive that statement, you need to *Balance the Account*. When you balance the account, you summarize all the transactions the bank has listed and compare them with the transactions you have in your Registry. The bank provides you with a form to use to do this on the back of your statement. It looks something like this:

BALANCE CHECKBOOK
Statement Date 02/26/05

1. Registry Balance	*$ 1,939.34*
2. Closing Amount on this statement	*$ 1,274.10*
3. Deposits you made Since Statement Close	*$ 1,763.88*
4. Total Lines 2 & 3	*$ 3,037.98*
5. Total Withdrawals not shown on Statement (see below)	*$ 1,098.64*
6. Subtract Line 5 from Line 4. This should Equal Line 1	*$ 1,939.34*

Total Withdrawals NOT on this statement:

Check #	*Amount*
98	*$ 650.00*
Auto	*$ 40.00*
99	*$ 55.12*
100	*$ 60.25*
ATM	*$ 20.00*
101	*$ 273.27*
	$ 1,098.64

Let's review the information in this example. Prior to your paycheck on 2/28, the bank issues their statement of your account. They indicate you have a balance of $1,274.10 including $0.10 of interest earned during this period. First, you should review the statement against your Registry and make sure all the items match up to the date the statement was issued. If there are items on your statement not in your Registry, you need to add them to the Registry. You can use the "Code" column of the Registry to check that all the items match. In this example, you had $0.10 of interest on your statement that was NOT in your Registry. So your Registry total is $1,939.24 + $0.10 or $1,939.34. Put that total on line 1 and enter the statement balance number, $1,247.10, on line 2.

Next, you need to "balance" the deposits and withdrawals entries you have made in your Registry since the bank statement was issued. For line 3, you only have one deposit that was your paycheck on 2/28. You add lines 2 & 3 to obtain line 4. For withdrawals, you have written checks 98, 99, 100, and 101, have an Auto Draft and have withdrawn $20 from the ATM. You list all these, add them up and put the total in line 5. You subtract line 5 from line 4 and put that amount in line 6 which should equal line 1. If it does, everything is fine – congratulations! If not, you need to go back through your Registry and find the error because the <u>amounts must match</u>. Oftentimes you will find that you misread your had writing or recorded a number wrong. I have spent several hours looking for a $0.18 imbalance only to find I had written $275.53 rather than $275.35 in my Registry. You may also use some software to help you balance your checkbook and manage the rest of your finances. We will discuss that more in Chapter 6.

Now, we need to discuss the "Auto" payment to Be-All Wireless Phones on 3/7 in the Registry. This is commonly referred to as an *Auto Draft* of your checking account. Many companies such as the electric utility, phone company, and gas company allow you to set up with them to have your bills paid electronically, <u>automatically</u> each month. This saves you the hassle of writing and mailing a check to pay your bills. However, once you set it up, it occurs automatically each month on the same day and you <u>cannot</u> avoid it so be sure your cash flow will be such that the Auto Draft does not cause you to overdraw your account.

You can set this up either by completing an ACH (Automated Clearing House) Form with the company or you can set it up to pay it electronically from your bank's website. When you fill out the ACH form you will be asked to include a voided check which is a blank check with the word VOID written all over it. Be sure to record the check number in your Registry and indicate it was VOID and the amount is $0. They will also ask you to write down on the ACH form the 9-digit routing code and your account number that are on the bottom of your check. It usually takes 1-2 payment cycles for it to get established. In the meantime, you send a regular check. Once the ACH is established, you may still receive a paper bill in the mail but it will say "Do Not Pay, Auto Draft" or something to that effect.

Another alternative is to have these types of transactions automatically charged to a credit card each month. Your bill paying can be extremely simplified if you can get all your monthly bills set up for Auto Draft on your credit card. I did this when I lived in Phoenix, Arizona. That way, I only had to write one check every month to my credit card company and eventually, with electronic funds transfer from my bank (EFT), I could transfer money from my bank to the credit card company over the internet. I didn't have to write *any* checks.

Doing this, I also knew that I would never get into an overdraft situation when any of my bills became due sine they were paid immediately by the credit card company. In addition, using the credit card helped improve my cash flow since I could maintain a higher daily balance in my checking account because I only had one major outflow each month. Finally, if I did get into trouble one month (not enough money to pay my bills), I could pay part of the credit card bill and catch up next month.

Unfortunately, not all companies are set up this way so the ACH may be the only way you can do Auto Draft with particular entities. Remember to be careful if you choose the credit card method because when you do not see the money going out of your account, it's easy to get into trouble. We will talk about Credit Cards a little later in this chapter but first we need to learn about some credit basics.

CREDIT BASICS

Establishing good credit is the single most important step you can take to secure a good financial future. Your credit rating will determine how much money banks will lend you, the interest rate you are charged and the limit for your credit cards. So how do you do this? Well, actually you are already on your way. Opening a Checking and Savings account is a good first step. By managing your money properly, paying your bills when they are due and not bouncing checks, you demonstrate over time that you are capable of handling your finances. When you decide you want to get a credit card or apply for a loan, you will have a track record that the credit card or loan company can review that demonstrates your ability.

One of the definitions for Credit in Webster's Dictionary is "Financial Trustworthiness." That's exactly what it is for you. When you have good credit, it means lending institutions like banks believe they can trust you and they are confident that if they lend you money, you will pay them back. But it is also important when you rent your first apartment (Chapter 7) or decide to buy your first car (Chapter 9). No one will rent you an apartment or loan you money for a car and allow you to pay them monthly if you do not have a good credit history. Well, they might, but you will pay a lot more for these things if you have bad credit.

The amount of credit you can obtain depends on a number of factors including your income, expenses, debts and of course your financial history. Remember that Volkswagen Beetle we discussed? What if your rent was $900 per month rather than $650? Do you think the bank would lend you the money to buy it? Probably not because based upon the other expense in our examples you would not have enough money each month to pay all your bills. What if you had a history of bouncing a check every 3 weeks? Again, why would they want to give you more money if you cannot manage the money you have?

So how does credit work? Basically, having credit means you can delay payment for something rather than having to pay for it all at once. Lending institutions want to insure that they only extend credit to individuals who are a good credit risk or in other words are highly likely to repay their debts. Let's talk about the VW Beetle again and say the car costs $21,000. If you want to buy it you either have to give them the entire $21,000 or you have to finance it through credit. From our previous example, Volkswagen Credit would have reviewed your financial situation and gathered information about you including your income, your job, the amount of time you had worked at your present employer, the debts you have and your monthly expenses. They then run a calculation to determine if you are worthy of a loan for $21,000.

If you have a really good track record you might get the loan with a 4% interest rate. If you have fair track record, you might still get the loan but the interest rate might be 9%. They charge a higher interest rate because it allows them to collect more money from you quicker. Also, the higher interest rate may make the monthly payment too high for you to afford. Either way, they are trying to protect themselves in the case that you are unable to may your payments. This is called being in *default* and you do NOT want this to ever happen.

Financial institutions, like Volkswagen Credit, rely upon three major companies to provide them with credit information about you and all their other customers. These three credit bureaus (Equifax, Experion and Trans Union) collect information about everyone who uses credit. They track your all your credit related accounts including credit cards, store credit cards, loans, bills, and on and on. They record information about any late payments you have had or when you have failed to pay at all. They look to see if you are opening new accounts frequently which usually means you are not managing the accounts you have and need new ones to "stay afloat." They use all this information to calculate what is called a *Credit Score.* The credit score is a universal number that any lending professional can use to determine your credit risk to their firm compared to other consumers.

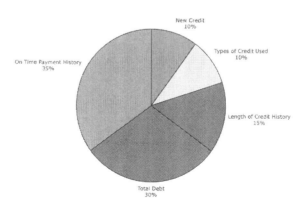

Each bureau has it own unique credit scores but more recently all three have begun to use what is called the *FICO® Score* named for the Fair Isaac Corporation that developed the models used to make the calculations. The FICO® scores range widely and the following chart from the www.MyFICO.com website shows the percentage of consumers that fall into each range:

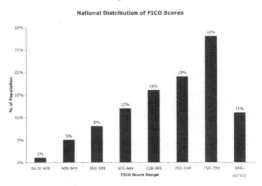

The FICO® Score uses five credit areas each weighted differently to determine the score:

PAYMENT HISTORY
- Account payment information on specific types of accounts (credit cards, retail accounts, installment loans, finance company accounts, mortgage, etc.)
- Presence of adverse public records (bankruptcy, judgements, suits, liens, wage attachments, etc.), collection items, and/or delinquency (past due items)
- Severity of delinquency (how long past due)
- Amount past due on delinquent accounts or collection items
- Time since (recency of) past due items (delinquency), adverse public records (if any), or collection items (if any)
- Number of past due items on file
- Number of accounts paid as agreed

TOTAL DEBT
- Amount owing on accounts
- Amount owing on specific types of accounts
- Lack of a specific type of balance, in some cases
- Number of accounts with balances

- Proportion of credit lines used (proportion of balances to total credit limits on certain types of revolving accounts)
- Proportion of installment loan amounts still owing (proportion of balance to original loan amount on certain types of installment loans)

LENGTH OF CREDIT HISTORY
- Time since accounts opened
- Time since accounts opened, by specific type of account
- Time since account activity

NEW CREDIT
- Number of recently opened accounts, and proportion of accounts that are recently opened, by type of account
- Number of recent credit inquiries
- Time since recent account opening(s), by type of account
- Time since credit inquiry(s)
- Re-establishment of positive credit history following past payment problems

TYPES OF CREDIT USED
- Number of (presence, prevalence, and recent information on) various types of accounts (credit cards, retail accounts, installment loans, mortgage, consumer finance accounts, etc.)

Again, as you can see, the best way to have a good credit score is to pay your bills on time and not over extend yourself with too much debt. The sooner you begin establishing credit the better and one great way to do that is with a credit card.

CREDIT CARDS
Credit cards are a truly wonderful invention. They allow you to acquire things with ease without having to carry large sums of cash or remembering to take you checkbook. However, every year, thousands of people get into trouble by overextending themselves with credit cards. It is not surprising in our on-demand society that such a problem exists but it is <u>completely avoidable</u> if people remember one simple rule – Never, NEVER, spend more money than you have unless it is an emergency. It sounds so simple. It IS so simple yet so many people

neglect this simple rule.

The credit card companies know this and they start their customers very young. When I was in college with <u>no job and no income</u> I received at least 3 offers every week asking me to sign up for another credit card. It was amazing. It's no wonder so many college students graduate in debt! It is just too easy. You sign up for the card. You go out to dinner with your friends and buy some stuff for your dorm room. You can't pay off the entire balance so you make the minimum payment. The credit card companies conveniently provide you with a simple minimum payment to make your life easier. Unfortunately, if you always make the minimum payment, the interest charges you accrue will cause your debt to mushroom into a size you have no hopes of controlling.

Before we go any further we need to clarify definitions. There is a major difference between a need and a want. You *need* to breath or you will die. You *want* that cheeseburger for lunch but you would be fine eating a sandwich packed from home. Reread those last two sentences. It is <u>crucial </u>that you clearly understand the difference if you do not want to become another bankruptcy statistic. Always be sure you are using your credit card only for what you need. If you want something, have the money for it <u>before</u> you charge it. I cannot stress enough how dangerous this little piece of plastic can be if you are not careful with it.

So, how does the credit card work? Well, first you have to get one. There are four major card issuers in the United States: VISA, Mastercard, Discover and American Express. All the cards allow you to make a minimum payment and "roll" the balance each month except American Express. Which one should you choose? Personally, I use Discover for most of my purchases because they give me a 1% rebate on every charge I make. So if I spend $10,000 a year on my card, I get a check for $100. That's $100 I didn't have so I gladly use the card. Unfortunately, there are still a few places that do not accept Discover so I also carry a VISA Card. It's the same VISA account my parents opened for me when I went to college over 20 years ago. That's it. Just two cards. I still get offers every week for more but I have stuck with those two cards and they have served me well. Any more than two would be trouble.

For a young person starting their financial life, I recommend getting only those same two cards: Discover and VISA. Using these wisely will allow you to establish some credit history. Various banks issue the VISA cards and many organizations (such as college alumni groups) offer "special" cards with a school logo or NASCAR driver and etc. You should first check with the bank with which you established your checking account to see what they offer. Remember, your VISA card should not be a debit card tied to your checking account but a stand-alone credit card. If it is lost or stolen, you have much more protection with a credit card than a debit card.

You want to be sure you get a card with no annual fees. Your initial credit limit or the amount you can charge to the card should be around $500-$1,000 for each of the cards. This will be enough credit for you to make some charges but not too much to get into trouble. After you have established some payment history with the card company, feel comfortable using the card and are sure you have the correct amount of discipline, you can always request a credit increase.

At the end of the month, the credit card company will send you a billing statement. It will show all the transactions you had for the last 30 days and the total amount you owe (along with that scary minimum payment amount). You need to compare the statement to your receipts to be sure there are not any unauthorized charges. If there are any discrepancies, you must contact your card company <u>immediately</u> and work to resolve them. If you do not, you could be liable for the charges and have to pay for things you did not purchase. Once all is in order, write a check to the card company and mail it in well in advance so you do not incur any late fees. As I mentioned previously, many card companies allow you to pay your bill on-line by linking the credit card company to your bank account. This is NOT an Auto Draft but saves you the hassle of trying to get the check in the mail on time. With on-line EFT, you can pay your bill anytime, night or day over the internet.

Another thing you need to realize is the merchant pays a fee for the credit card service. It is typically 2-3% of the purchase price. So, for example, if you buy a new iPod for $100 with your credit card, the store gets $98 and $2 goes to the credit card company. The store is willing to do this because they receive their cash immediately so they are willing to "discount" the price in this manner. One of the reasons Discover is not accepted as widely as VISA and Mastercard is Discover's fee is higher (how did you think that 1% they give back was created?).

The cash flow benefits for you are very similar. By using your credit card for all you purchases, you have established 30-day payment terms with everyone. You do not have to pay for that new iPod player now; you pay at the end of the month. If you are tight on cash now but will have more cash with your paycheck at the end of the month, you get to enjoy the new iPod player all that much sooner. Also, using the credit card provides you an itemized statement each month identifying where your money is going. This can help you refine your budget and make the most of your financial plan. You might also choose to use some software to manage your finances. We will discuss that more in Chapter 6. In the meantime, we need to talk about how you borrow money.

LOANS

For most things you purchase, you should be able to manage your money so that you can pay for the item immediately or at least when the credit card statement arrives. This is because the majority of your purchases are items that cost little relative to your income. However, when you decide to purchase a car or a house, the amount of money required is so high that you will most likely not have enough saved to pay with cash. Therefore, you will need to obtain a loan.

A loan is a contract that is established between you and a financial institution. Oftentimes this is a bank but it could also be the finance department of the automobile company from whom you purchase your car or another firm that specializes only in loans and does not offer other banking services like checking accounts. Either way, the financial institution will agree to give you all the money you need to purchase the expensive item you desire and even allow you to repay the money over several years on a monthly basis. However, for this privilege, they charge you *interest* which is a fee for "use" of their money over this period of time. This makes it very easy for you to fit an expensive item into your budget but be careful; there are many traps along the way.

PAYMENTS AND INTEREST

There are two methods to calculate the interest charged on a loan; *Simple and Compound.* Simple Interest is taking the amount you are borrowing, multiplying by an interest rate and determining the "fee" or interest you will be charged. The interest rate you are charged depends on several factors including the current Federal Funds Rate, your credit history and the length of time you will borrow the money. As we discussed in Credit Basics, be sure to maintain a good credit history so you can get the best rate available.

Let's review an example. If you borrow $20,000 for a car, agree to pay it back in 5 years and are charged 7% simple interest, your interest charge (oftentimes called your *Finance Charge*) would be $20,000 * 0.07 or $1,400. You add this to the $20,000 you borrowed and that is the total amount you owe the bank. To determine your monthly payment you take the total amount owed and divide by the total months you take to repay the money (called the *Life of the Loan*). So in this example it would be $21,400 ÷ 60 payments = $356.67. It's pretty simple so of course this is not the method the bank uses.

Compound Interest is the method used by every financial institution. Compound interest is calculated based upon the *Time Value of Money* that compensates the bank for the changes in the value of money over time due to inflation. Remember when we discussed inflation in Chapter 2? If the bank loans you money over a five year period, the dollars you pay back in year one may be worth more than the dollars in year five. The bank does not want to receive dollars that are worth less over time so they adjust for this situation by using the compound interest formula:

$$Monthly\ Payment = PV*\{[R*(1+R)^N] \div [(1+R)^{N}-1]\}$$

PV = Present Value of the money or the amount you want to borrow;
R = Interest Rate you are charged divided by the number of compounding periods;
N = The number of periods in the loan or the number of payments you will make.

This means you are charged interest every month on the amount of the loan you still have outstanding. So let's do an example using our car loan.

PV = $20,000
R = 0.07÷12 (Again, the rate divided by the number of compounding periods).
N = 5 years x 12 months = 60 periods or 60 payments.

$$Monthly\ Payment = \$20,000*\{[0.00583*(1+0.00583)^{60}] \div [(1+0.00853)^{60}-1]\}$$
$$= \$20,000* [0.00826 \div 0.4173]$$
$$= \$20,000* [0.01981]$$
$$\sim \$396.02$$

As you can see, "plugging" the variables into this equation will give you an answer but it is much easier to use a financial calculator or a spreadsheet program like Microsoft Excel® to calculate the payment terms (Go to www.RL101HANDBOOK.com for examples). Practice a few times with some known information. You might also ask to borrow the details about your parent's car loan and use that data to make sure you are doing the calculations properly.

Most finance institutions publish their interest rates as the Annual Percentage Rate or APR and this is the figure used in their loan calculations. Just always remember that whatever annual interest rate you are being charged, you need to divide that by the number of payments you will be making during each year (for most of us that means divide by 12). So your 7% interest rate is actually 0.583% per month and you will make 60 payments. Here's some more numbers about our same car loan:

Car Loan Example

Interest Type	*Compound*	*Simple*	*Difference*
Loan Amount	$ 20,000.00	$ 20,000.00	-
Time Period (Years)	5	5	-
Interest Rate	7%	7%	-
Monthly Payment	$ 396.02	$ 356.67	$ 39.36
Total Payments	$ 23,761.44	$ 21,400.00	$ 2,361.44
Finance Charge	$ 3,761.44	$ 1,400.00	$ 2,361.44

So essentially, because the bank is using Compound Interest, they are charging you interest each month for the entire amount of money you still owe them instead of just charging a lump sum interest payment as is done with simple interest. Using this method the $20,000 car now cost you $23,761.44 which is $39.36 more per month and $2,361.44 more total than it would be using simple interest.

Let me make this point another way. The payment you make each month on a Compound Interest Loan includes amounts for both the *principle and interest.* Principle is the amount that is being used to pay off the original amount of the loan (the Present Value) and interest is the fee charged by the bank for lending you the money. The monthly payment you make includes both these numbers added together. Also, a greater portion of your payment is towards interest in the beginning. Here's that same $20,000 loan with the $396.02 monthly payment broken out so you can see what I mean:

Payment	*Interest*	*Principle*	*% Payment that is Interest*
1	$116.67	$279.36	29.5%
2	$115.04	$280.99	29.0%
3	$113.40	$282.63	28.6%
4	$111.75	$284.27	28.2%
5	$110.09	$285.93	27.8%
6	$108.42	$287.60	27.4%
7	$106.75	$289.28	27.0%
8	$105.06	$290.97	26.5%
9	$103.36	$292.66	26.1%
10	$101.65	$294.37	25.7%
11	$99.94	$296.09	25.2%
12	$98.21	$297.81	24.8%
13	$96.47	$299.55	24.4%
14	$94.72	$301.30	23.9%
15	$92.97	$303.06	23.5%

16	$91.20	$304.82	23.0%
17	$89.42	$306.60	22.6%
18	$87.63	$308.39	22.1%
19	$85.83	$310.19	21.7%
20	$84.02	$312.00	21.2%
21	$82.20	$313.82	20.8%
22	$80.37	$315.65	20.3%
23	$78.53	$317.49	19.8%
24	$76.68	$319.34	19.4%

As you can see, over time more of your payment goes towards paying off the principle of the loan but in the beginning almost 30% of your loan payment is just in interest!

There is one way that you could reduce the amount of interest you pay and that is to pay the loan off early. If on that same 5 year loan, you paid off the loan in 3 years, you would save $1,529.23 in interest. Don't believe me? Run the calculation again changing the loan term from 5 years to 3 years or 36 payments and leave everything else the same.

Payoff Car Loan Early

Loan Amount	$ 20,000.00
Actual Time Period (Years)	3
Interest Rate	7%
Total Amount Owed (TOA) – 3 years	$ 22,231.51
Finance Charge – 3 years	$ 2,231.51
Total Monthly Payments (TMP)	$ 14,256.72
3 of 5 years or 36 payments @ $396.02	
Payoff Amount (TOA – TMP)	$ 7,974.79
Interest saved	$ 1,529.93

If you only borrow the money for three years, the bank will charge you less total interest since you borrowed the money for a shorter period of time. The only catch is you have to have enough money to payoff the loan early (in this case almost $8,000). If you call the bank, they will tell you what your exact payoff amount will be and that payoff amount will only be "good" for a certain period of time (again, Time Value of Money at work here) so you will have to have the funds ready to pay it off within 7-10 days after they give you an amount. You may want to do this for a few reasons such as reducing the interest you have to pay, refinancing the loan with another loan company to obtain a lower interest rate for the same time period or to make your interest payments tax deductible by using a Home Equity Loan (which we will discuss shortly).

Be careful! Some lenders charge a penalty for paying off your loan early. After all, they were counting on making all that money off you over that 5 years and now you want to take it away from them. So be sure to read the fine print on your loan and be sure there are no penalties for paying it off early. If there are, find another place to get the loan – you do not want to do business with any place that is that inflexible.

This brings me to another important point about your personal finances. **<u>NEVER SIGN ANYTHING THAT YOU DO NOT COMPLETELY UNDERSTAND.</u>** Once you sign that piece of paper, you are on the hook to adhere to the terms outlined in that document – period. If you do not understand something, ask for an explanation. If you do not like the explanation or still do not understand it, do not sign it. Also ask if you can have a copy of the document to have someone else review. If they refuse to let you take it, GET OUT OF THERE – those folks cannot be trusted and you will get screwed if you do any business with them. Loans are big decisions in your financial life so be sure you understand and agree with everything in the contract before you sign.

FIXED AND VARIABLE RATES

Now, there are some more things we need to discuss about using the Compound Interest method. In Compound Interest calculations, there are two ways in which the interest rate could be applied; a *Fixed Rate* or a *Variable Rate*. The examples we used for the car loan used a Fixed Rate that is the interest rate remained the same for the entire loan period. Most car loans and loans for similar personal property (like boats, motorcycles, etc.) work this way. Home loans on the other hand can also be Variable Rate Loans. In the home lending business they are called Adjustable Rate Mortgages or ARMs.

In an ARM, the interest rate is fixed for a certain period of time and then it fluctuates each year thereafter. So on a 7 year ARM, the rate would be fixed for the first 7 years and then change starting with the 8th year. Some ARMs allow the bank to change the rate 4 times (quarterly) during each year starting with the 8th year. These variable rates are usually tied to the Prime Lending Rate published in the Wall Street Journal. So your ARM may be set at Prime plus 3% so if the Prime rate is 5%, you would pay 8%. This could be dangerous for your budget if the Prime Rate continues to rise so it is wiser to choose a fixed rate loan.

However, the interest rates charged for ARMs are usually less than the fixed rate (Time Value of Money again) so your monthly payment will be less in the beginning during the fixed portion of the loan. It can be a good strategy for a first time home buyer to select a variable rate loan if he/she plans to only live in the house for a few years and knows the house will be sold before the variable rate takes affect. There are a lot of factors to consider before employing this strategy so be sure to read Chapter 10 very carefully so you do not get trapped!

HOME EQUITY LOAN

In Chapters 9 and 10 respectively, I will discuss the specifics of the loan process for buying a car and a home. However, there is one additional type of loan that I should mention now and that is the *Home Equity Loan*. This is a 2nd mortgage or loan where you borrow money using the equity in your home as collateral. *Equity* is the cash value you have built in your home and *Collateral* is anything of value you can use to *secure* a loan or, in other words, give the lender the right to take it should you default on the loan. So a Home Equity loan is when the bank loans you money using the amount of equity you have in your home as collateral. For example, let's say you have a home loan, also called the *Primary Mortgage,* with the following conditions:

- Purchase price of the house - $150,000;
- Down Payment 20% or $30,000;
- 6.00% fixed interest rate;
- 30 year loan duration;
- Monthly payment is $719.46 (practice and see if you can calculate this);
- Payments have been made for 2 years.

With these conditions, you have around $33,000 in equity in your home that you could use for the loan. This amount is the $30,000 down payment plus the $3,000 in principle payments you have made over the two years. The bank can provide you with a Home Equity Line of Credit up to that amount and you could use it to pay off other loans or improve your house or whatever. If you used the Home Equity Line to pay off your car loan early, you could save quite a bit of money since the Home Equity Line rates are usually (but not always) lower that the rates charged for car loans. In addition, interest charged for home mortgages or home equity loans is deductible from your income taxes whereas the interest on a car loan is not. So not only would you save money in the total interest you paid, you would also reduce the taxes you have to pay to Uncle Sam.

Many people across the United States have used home equity loans to pay off credit card debt and get themselves back into good financial shape. Just always be sure that when you do use one of these loans, you have a plan how you will repay the money because, after all, you borrowed it from yourself! Also, if you choose to sell you home, any amount due on the home equity loan must be paid off before the house is sold. This can be done at time the house is sold (called the *Closing*) and it simply reduces the amount of money you receive for the sale of the home. If we use the above example here is how it might look:

Home Equity Line Adjustment

Sale Price of Home	$ 155,000.00
Payoff Amount (after 2 years)	$ 116,961.88
Home Equity Balance	$ 10,000.00
Net Due to Seller	$ 28,038.12

Wait a minute! Didn't you put $30,000 down on the house and sell it for $5,000 more than you paid for it? Why are you only getting $28,038 back? You have sold the house for $5,000 more than when you bought it two years ago and you have paid the $120,000 loan down to $116,961. Remember the $719.46 monthly payment was principle and interest so only the principle amount added to you equity amount. That leaves you with $38,038 in "profit". Nevertheless, since you still owe $10,000 on your home equity line, it too has to be deducted. Overall you came out ok but this calculation does not include all the other fees that are paid by the seller during the sale of a home. We will discuss all that in much more detail in Chapter 10. Generally, the home equity line can be a very helpful tool to help you reduce interest expenses and taxes or to pay for that special vacation you want or the new furniture you need. Just be careful not to get in over your head.

One final comment about loans. You will be bombarded with offers from retailers to open a credit card account with them to get 0% financing and no payments for 90 days or perhaps even as long as a year. They want to "help" you afford everything from lawn mowers to arm chairs. Again, be very careful with these offers. What they do not tell you is that if you do not pay the balance off before the "no interest" period expires, they will charge you interest for the <u>entire period</u> and many times it is at a rate of over 20%! I admit that I have purchased things under plans such as these but I always paid them off before the year was over.

Have you ever heard the saying "Buyer Beware?" The way to stay out of trouble is to follow your financial plan. Loans are just another tool you can use to manage your financial life. Remember that they are just that – tools – use them to do what you want them to do and do not get trapped into financial problems because you allowed the tools to "manage" you. You have to decide for yourself if the loan you seek is for a need or a want and make an informed decision about what to do. The best way to keep yourself on track is to create and follow a budget.

Chapter 6 - Setting Up a Budget

IN THIS CHAPTER, we will discuss how to develop a budget to help you meet your financial goals. Before we develop the budget, we need to learn a bit more about some important financial statements you will need to use to measure your progress towards you goals.

FINANCIAL STATUS REPORTS

Earlier, we mentioned three major financial reports: The Balance Sheet, Income Statement and Cash Flow Statement. These three financial measurement reports will help you understand your own finances as well as the financial well being of any business as you will see in Chapter 11.

BALANCE SHEET

The *Balance Sheet* is a statement of ownership. If you have ever heard someone discuss calculating their *Net Worth*, they were discussing their balance sheet. The balance sheet lists all of the assets, liabilities and equity for a particular individual or business entity. When you are born, you have "0" in all these categories; you don't own anything and you don't owe anything to anybody. As you grow up, you accumulate things like clothes, toys, money from birthdays, allowance payments, etc. As you establish relationships with other people, circumstances arise that cause you to owe them something like a favor or some money you borrowed to buy a drink from the vending machine. This is what your balance sheet shows; everything you own along with everything you owe. Subtracting what you owe from what you own is your Net Worth and it can be positive (i.e. you own more than you owe) or negative (i.e. you owe more than you own).

So, let's start with some definitions. *Assets* are items that are owned that are cash or could be sold to obtain cash such as a car, a house, artwork, other personal property, or investments. It is the sum of all of all the liquid and non-liquid items in which you have an ownership stake. *Liquid* items are cash and anything that can become cash quickly such as savings bonds. *Non-Liquid* items are things that can become cash but take time to convert such as a car (you will not sell it the first day you list it for sale), a house, stocks and CDs (Certificates of Deposit – a savings instrument offered by banks that pays you interest for the use of your money. Once you give the bank your money, you usually have to wait 6 months or more before you can get it back with interest). The longer it takes to convert an item to cast the *less* liquid it is.

Liabilities are debts that you owe and for most people these are limited to credit cards and loans for items such as a car, a house, an educational loan, etc. *Equity* is what is left over after subtracting the liabilities from the assets. This follows the fundamental rule of accounting:

$$\text{Assets} = \text{Liabilities} + \text{Equity}$$

This must always be true. No exceptions. The assets must always equal the liabilities and the equity. Period.

Now, let's go back to the analogy of your personal life. Here's what a balance sheet for a 12 year old might look like:

Assets

Piggy Bank	$ 135.00
Total Current Assets	$ 135.00
Bike	$ 52.00
Video Game System (Nitron 2000)	$ 125.00
Skates	$ 45.00
Money given to friend for lunch	$ 6.00
Total Assets	**$ 363.00**

Liabilities

Money Borrowed for Soda	$ 1.00
New Video Game on Dad's Credit Card	$ 29.95
Overdue Library Book Charges	$ 12.00
Total Current Liabilities	$ 42.95
Loan from parents for Nitron 2000	$ 120.00
Total Liabilities	**$ 162.95**
Total Net Worth	**$ 200.05**

As you can see, this kid is in pretty good shape. At 12 years old, she has a positive net worth! She also has a loan for her video game system the Nitron 2000. Every time you take out a loan, you also have an asset for the item that your are buying over time. In this example, we are assuming the no-interest loan was made for 10 months at $12.50 per month and she has made one payment of $5.00 towards the loan. Since her allowance is $5 per week, she will still have $8.50 per month for other expenses. This example is extremely over simplified and does not include things like depreciation which we will discuss later but you get the idea.

Two other things to notice are the lines *Total Current Assets* and *Total Current Liabilities*. The word "current" refers to items that are very liquid (again like cash) when discussing assets and items that are due relatively soon when discussing liabilities. Another calculation to make is something called the *Current* Ratio which is determined by dividing Current Assets by Current Liabilities. For this youngster, the ratio is 3.14 meaning she has 3 times her current liabilities in current assets.

Of course, the higher the ratio or absolute number the better. A ratio of "1" means you have the same amount of each. A ratio lower than "1" means that for your immediate situation you owe more than you have which, unfortunately, is the case for far to many people in this country. You should always strive to have a Current Ratio higher than "1" or a *Positive Current Net Worth*.

Do not confuse the Current Net Worth with your Total Net Worth. Most Americans have a negative Total Net Worth and it is not necessarily a bad thing. You may be a financial dynamo and have $50,000 of positive net worth when you graduate college. However, as soon as you buy a house and a car, you will be just like everybody else – owing more than you have. The key is to continue to build your assets so you can get to a position where even though you have a house and a car loan, you own more assets than those loans!

Assets

Bank and Cash Accounts

National Bank Checking	$	27,642.89
Vanguard Money Market Account	$	18,250.00
Total Current Assets	$	45,892.89

Other Assets

Lake Property	$	11,100.00
Primary Residence	$	355,000.00
Total Other Assets	$	366,100.00

Investment Accounts

Thomas & Anne's Joint Investments	$	117,425.14
Tom's 401(k)	$	279,542.65
Vanguard Bond Account	$	467,842.11
Vanguard Investments	$	551,247.42
Total Investments	$	1,416,057.32

Total Assets	**$**	**1,828,050.21**

Liabilities
Credit Cards

Previous card (No longer used)	$	984.25
Discover Credit Card	$	4,500.00
VISA Platinum Card	$	836.00
Total Current Liabilities	$	6,320.25

Loans

Home Loan	$	185,587.04
Mercedes Loan	$	42,584.00
BMW SUV Loan	$	52,694.00
Total Loans	$	280,865.04

Total Liabilities	**$**	**287,185.29**
Total Net Worth	**$**	**1,540,864.92**

Above is a typical balance sheet from a imaginary 50 year old couple. They are a dual income household making over $70,000 a year. As you can see from their Total Net Worth, they have done well to manage their finances and save as much money as possible. While they have a fairly high level of credit card debt, it is not unmanageable for their income (what is their Current Ratio?).

As I mentioned, your balance sheet will not look that strong when you first start out. In fact, you will probably have a negative Total Net Worth. If we pull some information from our previous examples, you owe $20,000 on your VW Beetle, owe $495 on your credit card and only have $1,900 in your checking account and no other assets or debt, your Total Net Worth is:

$$\$1,900 - \$20,000 - \$495 = \$(17,605)$$

In accounting the parenthesis () represents a negative number. So now you start to panic. You're thinking "I owe $20,495 dollars and I can't pay for that because I only have $1,900; I'm going bankrupt!" Not quite. There is a difference between having enough money to pay off all your debt and having enough money to pay your bills when they are due. This is where the Cash Flow and Income Statements become important.

INCOME & CASH FLOW STATEMENTS

The *Income Statement* identifies the amount of money you have remaining after subtracting your income from your expenses over a given period of time. You should review this on a monthly basis. If you are running a business or reviewing the financial statements of a business for investment purposes (like in Chapter 11), the Income and Cash Flow Statements are different. For individuals, they are the same.

Here is why. Businesses operate on what is called an *Accrual* basis where individuals operate on a *Cash* basis. What's the difference? Well, generally businesses will extend each other credit where individuals have to pay for goods or services when they are received. For example, let's say Bob's Rental Company needs some office supplies. Bob's purchasing department places an order for certain items (pens, paper clips, paper, staples, etc.) and a few days later it receives those items from Sally's Office Supply. Sally's store issues Bob's Rental Company an invoice for $150.29 that says 1%-10, Net 30. This means if Bob's Rental Company chooses to pay the bill in 10 days, they can take a discount of 1% ($1.50 in this case) off of their bill or they can pay the total amount in 30 days. Most companies will choose to wait the 30 days to conserve their cash (remember our credit card discussion?).

At the time Sally's store ships the products, they record a sale (income) for $150.29 on their income statement and add an asset to their balance sheet of the same amount that is owed to them by Bob's Rental Company. Bob's Rental Company records an expense for office supplies on their Income statement and a liability on their balance sheet for $150.29 - the amount they owe Sally's Company. Sales and expenses are recorded when they occurred but no cash has changed hands.

Now, if you go to Sally's store, you will have to pay the $150.29 for those same items when you check out. You will not get to wait 30 days to pay for them. Essentially, in Accrual based systems, there is time between when revenue or expenses are recorded and when the cash actually changes hands. In Cash based systems, it all happens at the same time.

Although you might not think so, reviewing the Income Statement, Balance Sheet and Cash Flow statements for a business can be quite confusing. There are situations when companies show positive income or profit but have negative cash flow. The reverse is also possible. Suffice to say that you must have a relatively good understanding of how these statements work to make an informed decision about whether to invest your money in a particular company.

We will discuss investing more in Chapter 11 but take this small piece of advice: Enroll in some accounting classes in college regardless of what you choose as major course of study. Be sure the classes will cover Basic Accounting and Financial Accounting. Review the course syllabus to insure you will be learning about these different accounting statements, how they work and how they are tied together. I wish I had done that in undergraduate school. If I had, I would have had knowledge about these key financial management tools 5 years earlier than I did.

Let's return to our sample Cash Flow Statement from Chapter 4.

Monthly Cash Flow Statement:	Amount
INCOME	
Total NET Monthly Income	$ 1,763.88
EXPENSES	
Place to Live (Apartment Rent)	$ 630.00
Food	$ 250.00
Auto Loan	$ 273.27
Utilities (Electric, Water, Natural Gas)	$ 125.87
Telephone	$ 40.24
Cable TV/Satellite	$ 45.99
Insurance (Auto)	$ 50.18
Insurance (Property)	$ 20.34
Gasoline	$ 100.00
Property Taxes on Car (Estimate based on SC Rates)	$ 37.50
Total Expenses	$ 1,573.39
Amount Remaining	$ 190.49

% EXPENSES as a percent of INCOME   89.20%

You now understand a little bit better what this report is telling you and you know that since you operate on a Cash based system, this is both your Income and Cash Flow Statement. This is telling you how you are doing each month. Are you generating enough cash? Do you need to cut back on your expenses? Are you ready to buy a house? Well, $190 a month is not that much *Free Cash Flow*, or money you have left over each month, to allow you to save for the future or "handle" the unexpected. However, this is not the "entire" picture. We need to also look at your assets and liabilities so let's add to this what your Balance Sheet might look like:

Assets

Checking Account	$	1,935.24
Total Current Assets	$	1,935.24
Vanguard Mutal Fund Investment	$	5,000.00
Vanguard Money Market Fund	$	2,500.00

Total Other Assets	$	7,500.00
Total Assets	$	**9,435.24**
Liabilities		
Discover Card	$	495.00
Total Current Liabilities	$	495.00
VW Bug Loan	$	20,011.23
Student Loan	$	2,546.81
Total Loans	$	22,558.04
Total Liabilities	$	**23,053.04**
Total Net Worth	$	**(13,617.80)**

Well, as we imagined, you have a negative Total Net Worth, which again, at this early stage of your financial life is not necessarily a bad thing. You have managed to keep your credit card under control and have a manageable balance. Your Current Ratio is 3.91 which is very strong. You also have managed to save and invest some money for the future. However, with your low monthly cash flow, it will be hard to continue to increase your assets.

The other thing to consider is how the value of your assets changes over time without you adding or subtracting any money from them. For example, you will drive your VW Bug each year and add mileage to the odometer. Would you be willing to pay the same amount for a car that has 12,000 miles as you would for one that has 15 miles on it? Of course not and neither would anyone else. Therefore, the VW Bug will *depreciate* over time (i.e. with each passing mile, the car is worth less than it was brand new). So while your loan balance for the car is $20,011.23, it may only be worth $19,611. If you sold the car, and could only get $19,000 for it, you would have to come up with the other ~$1,000 to pay off the loan. Some assets like a house or stocks can increase in value over time or *appreciate.* The point is you have to be aware that the value of the items you own can change and how it affects your overall financial plan.

TARGET EXPENSE PERCENTAGES

Here are some suggested percentage guidelines based on net income compiled by Dave Ramsey, author of *Financial Peace*. In his book Mr. Ramsey indicates these are only recommended percentages and will change dramatically if you have a very high or very low income.

Recommended Expenses as a % of Income

	Lower	*Upper*
Housing	25.0%	35.0%
Utilities	5.0%	10.0%
Food	5.0%	15.0%
Transportation	10.0%	15.0%
Clothing	2.0%	7.0%
Medical/Health	5.0%	10.0%
Debts	5.0%	10.0%
Total Basics	57.0%	102.0%
Charitable Gifts	10.0%	15.0%
Saving	5.0%	10.0%
Personal	5.0%	10.0%
Recreation	5.0%	10.0%
Total Others	25.0%	45.0%

Now let's compare the expenses from our cash flow statement to Mr. Ramsey's recommendations:

Monthly Expenses

	Amount	*Actual*	*Lower*	*Upper*
Housing	$ 630.00	35.7%	25.0%	35.0%
Food	$ 250.00	14.2%	5.0%	15.0%
Debt (Car Payment)	$ 273.27	15.5%	5.0%	10.0%
Utilities	$ 212.10	12.0%	5.0%	10.0%
(Elec, Gas, Phone, Cable)				
Personal (Taxes & Insurance)	$ 108.02	6.1%	5.0%	10.0%
Transportation (Gas)	$ 100.00	5.7%	10.0%	15.0%
Total Net Monthly Income	$ 1,763.88			
Total Expenses	$ 1,573.39			
Amount Remaining	$ 190.49			
% EXPENSES/INCOME		89.2%	55.0%	95.0%

Although the overall % of expense to income is within the Lower and Upper ranges he establishes, for this situation the overall percentage should be much closer to the lower number. The upper range is for people who are making considerably more money than in our example. In fact, for both housing and debt, we are over the recommended maximums. So we need to evaluate where the money is being spent and how we can reduce those expenses to provide more money for savings.

SAVE FIRST

You may have heard people say that the best way to save money is to "pay yourself first." This is very true. Each month you will have bills to pay so why not set up a "bill" to pay yourself? It's really quite simple when you think about it. By building that savings "bill" into your budget, you will force yourself to save for the future. In fact, if you set up an automatic deposit for your savings it is even better as there will be less temptation to use that money for other reasons during the month. Why should you do this? Again, it's compound interest.

When you save money you are doing in reverse what the bank does when they lend you money. Remember in our previous examples how much more you were charged in interest using compound interest rather than simple interest? Well the same is true when you save. And the sooner you start, the more money you will have.

An example will be very helpful. Suppose you decide to save $100 each month for 10 years and then stop contributing after the 10th year. Let's compare that to waiting ten years and then saving $100 each month for the last 10 years. We will also assume you can get a 6% interest rate on your money because you have invested it in a conservative growth mutual fund. Here's what the numbers look like:

Savings Comparison

Year	Monthly Savings	Total Saved	Monthly Savings	Total Saved
1	$ 100.00	$ 1,233.56	-	$ 0
2	$ 100.00	$ 2,543.20	-	$ 0
3	$ 100.00	$ 3,933.61	-	$ 0
4	$ 100.00	$ 5,409.78	-	$ 0
5	$ 100.00	$ 6,977.00	-	$ 0
6	$ 100.00	$ 8,640.89	-	$ 0
7	$ 100.00	$ 10,407.39	-	$ 0

8	$ 100.00	$ 12,282.85	-		$ 0
9	$ 100.00	$ 14,273.99	-		$ 0
10	$ 100.00	$ 16,387.93	$	100.00	$ 1,233.56
11	$ -	$ 17,398.71	$	100.00	$ 2,543.20
12	$ -	$ 18,471.82	$	100.00	$ 3,933.61
13	$ -	$ 19,611.12	$	100.00	$ 5,409.78
14	$ -	$ 20,820.69	$	100.00	$ 6,977.00
15	$ -	$ 22,104.87	$	100.00	$ 8,640.89
16	$ -	$ 23,468.25	$	100.00	$ 10,407.39
17	$ -	$ 24,915.72	$	100.00	$ 12,282.85
18	$ -	$ 26,452.47	$	100.00	$ 14,273.99
19	$ -	$ 28,084.00	$	100.00	$ 16,387.93
20	$ -	$ 29,816.15	$	100.00	$ 18,632.26

Net Increase Savings   *$11,183.89!*

This is the power of compound interest. The total you invest in each case is $100 x 12 months x 10 years or $12,000 but by starting now you save over $11,000 more than if you wait and make $1,200 more in contributions 10 years later! There is no more powerful example for why you should always pay yourself first and stick to it. When you decide to buy a car or a house, you will have the money you need for a down payment, closing costs, etc. And the more money you save each month, the larger that total amount saved becomes!

Where should you put this money you are saving? Your best bet is in some type of mutual fund that will provide a better return that a regular bank account but there are risks associated with investing. We will discuss that in detail in Chapter 11.

FINANCIAL MANAGEMENT SOFTWARE

Finally, there are a few pieces of software on the market that can help you manage your personal finances. The two most popular are Microsoft Money® and Quicken® by Intuit. Either software will allow you to manage all your accounts including your checking, savings, credit cards, investments, and loans. They also provide useful reports to create your income/cash flow statements and balance sheets. You can even set up all your bills and establish a budget.

I am not going to recommend one particular type of software. You can visit each company's website, evaluate them for yourself and choose whichever one is the most comfortable for you. Just be sure to do it. For the first five years of my life that I was on my own, I did not use software. One of the software packages was included with a new personal computer I purchased. After I entered the data into the software, I was amazed how much I had already fouled up my financial situation. Within a year of using the software and analyzing the reports it provided, I was able to get control of my expenses and had positive cash flow each month.

Chapter 7 - Finding a Place to Live

NOW THAT YOU are a financial dynamo, you are ready to find your own place to live. However, just like everything else we've discussed, there are many twists and turns you need to know before you go driving full speed down this road. For most of us, our first place that is "our own" is something that we rent from its actual owner. This could be an apartment, a spare bedroom over someone's garage or a house. But why? Why not just buy your first place and skip the whole "renting" process?

RENT VS. OWN

The reason most people's first "home" is rented is very simple – money. To purchase a home, you must have enough money for a down payment which is cash you must pay at the time you purchase the house. The minimum amount to use for a down payment is 5% and the traditional standard is 20%. That means if you are purchasing a $150,000 house you will need between $7,500 and $30,000 for a down payment. There are additional *Closing Costs* that you will also have to pay to purchase a home such as attorney, inspection and loan fees. Suffice to say most of us do not have that amount of money available to us upon graduation from college. If you do and you are ready to buy your first home, good for you. You'll find all the details you need to consider in Chapter 10. For the rest of us, we need to discuss how to secure our first home through the rental process.

RENTING

Renting is just what it sounds like. You pay someone a specified amount each month for the privilege of "using" his or her property as your home. That's it – sort of. To rent an apartment, you must sign a leasing contract that spells out all the things you agree to do and all the things the owner (or landlord) agrees to do. This will probably be the first contract you ever sign in your life. It will identify your monthly rent payment, what utilities are included (if any), what you must do to maintain the apartment, when the landlord can enter your apartment, how disputes are handles and numerous other *Terms and Conditions* or "rules" in the contract. I mentioned this in Chapter 5 but it bears repeating:

DO NOT SIGN ANYTHING THAT YOU DO NOT FULLY UNDERSTAND!

The best thing to do when shopping for your first apartment is to visit several places and determine which 2 or 3 you like the most. Ask for a copy of their leasing agreement and take it home and study it. If they will not let you take a copy, that's a bad sign and get away from that place and don't look back. After you've read the contract, if you do not understand something, ask someone for help. If you do not have someone to help you, find an attorney and have him review the contracts with you. It may cost you some additional money to get the assistance of an attorney but it is much better than signing a 12 month contract without fully understanding it and getting in a bad situation. The best way to find an attorney is NOT the television ads or yellow pages. Talk to people you know and get a recommendation. That will get you moving (pun intended) in the right direction.

Once you have weeded through all the contractual issues and determined which apartment is best for you, arrange a tour of the apartment complex. Have them show you some of the exact places they have available not just their model apartment. The model apartment is usually decorated complete with furnishings and will look very appealing. You want to see one that has been used in the past to see how well they maintain their units and how they prepare them for new tenants. Also check the showers, sinks and toilets for stains or signs of abnormal wear. Turn all the faucets and showers on and off and test to see that there are not any leaks and that the hot water works. Lastly, look at the kitchen appliances (stove, refrigerator, microwave, dishwasher) and inspect these for their condition. How do you know if they are in good condition? Well, how do they compare to the one's in your parent's house? Also ask about the age of the appliances and the process to replace them if a problem is discovered later. In most cases, the landlord will be responsible to provide these items.

Check if there is a washer and dryer hookup in the unit. You may not be able to afford a washer and dryer now but when you're ready, you want to be able to hook them up. Be sure to ask about their maintenance staff. How many people are on staff? What are their normal hours? Are they around on weekends? How do you contact them during an emergency? Keep in mind that if you have a problem and the maintenance staff needs to repair it, they may come into your apartment during the week when you are at work or school. Be sure you know what day and time that is supposed to happen and have your apartment "secured" so you do not temp them with easily stolen items (e.g. gold ring laying on top of your dresser). It is a good idea to inspect your apartment when you return to make sure the work was performed and that nothing is missing. Report any problems to the landlord immediately. Finally, see if you can speak to some of the current tenants at the complex and find out how they like living there.

There are many start-up costs you will incur. First there will still be a down payment you will have to make which is customarily equal to one month's rent (much smaller than what's required for a house!). So figure on paying two times your rent payment just to get into the place. Next, you have to get all your utilities connected. These fall into two categories: Necessities (electricity, phone and natural gas) and luxuries (Cable TV, High Speed Internet, etc.).

Utility companies charge a fee to connect your services. In addition, they may require a deposit if you do not have sufficient credit history to demonstrate you pay your bills on time. You can sometimes get around the deposit requirement by agreeing to have your bill automatically drafted against your checking account or charged to a credit card. Finally, they will require some proof that you reside at the address for which you are requesting service. Most times, a copy of the lease agreement is enough to prove you live where you say you do.

Be smart about what services you get connected. If you are like me and use your cell phone for all of your phone needs, you can avoid having the phone connected and save both the connection and monthly fees. If you know you want high speed internet and cable, you do not have to get them connected right away but if your budget allows, then go ahead. There's that word again...budget. That's right. You should do some homework *before* you sign the lease agreement to determine how much money you will need to get into your new place. When you get the contract, also ask for the list of utility companies you would need to contact. Call the utility companies and find out what they charge for connection fees, what deposits are required, etc. and develop your moving budget. You might do something like this:

Moving Budget

	Initial Fee	Deposit	Total
Apartment Rent	$ 650.00	$ 650.00	$ 1,300.00
Electricity	$ 55.00	$ 100.00	$ 155.00
Natural Gas	$ 70.00	$ 100.00	$ 170.00
Cable TV	$ 50.00	$ 75.00	$ 125.00
Phone	$ 100.00	$ -	$ 100.00

Total Necessity	$ 1,625.00
Total Luxury	$ 225.00
Grand Total	$ 1,850.00

As you can see, you still need quite a bit of money just to move into your first apartment. Developing this budget will help you determine the minimum amount of money you will need. In fact, you might want to do some of this research a year before you plan to start renting to give you time to save more money if you need to do so.

But utilities and rent are not all the only expenses you will have when you move. You will also need to move your stuff. If you cannot do it with your own vehicle or ones you can borrow from friends or family, you will need to rent a truck. There will be another contract you will need to review. In addition, you will need to shop the major rental companies (Ryder, Penske, Hertz and Uhaul) to determine who has the best rate and value for your situation. Depending upon how far you are moving and how much stuff you have this could cost you another $100 or more so do your homework.

Finally, you will need to consider if your budget will allow you to purchase a washer and dryer or if you will need to wait and use the Laundromat for a while. I used the Laundromat in my first apartment and was able to purchase a washer and dryer when I decided to move a year later. I had that washer and dryer set for almost 14 years. A good set will cost you from $800 to $1,500 so again, shop around and find the best deal for your situation. Then, plan your budget so you can make the purchase (Is that $196 of free cash flow from our example still looking good?).

Now that you have selected the place, moved and begun your new life there's one more thing you need: insurance.

Chapter 8 - Insurance

INSURANCE is a critical part of your financial plan. It protects you should the unexpected happen by paying to repair or replace items of yours that have been damaged. Insurance can be very complicated so we need to understand some basic terms before we proceed.

Liability is the term that is used to define who is responsible for the "problem". If you accidentally start a fire in your apartment and the building burns to the ground, you are responsible or liable for the damage. Insurance protects you against this liability by collecting a fee from you each month *in case* you have a problem. Everyone else who has a policy with that insurance company is doing the same thing and the theory is that not everyone who pays will have an accident at the same time. So, you are paying a monthly fee to the insurance company and they are using it to pay *Claims,* the requests for money under the terms of the insurance contract, from their other customers. Here are the typical steps in the insurance process:

1. Customer identifies need for insurance;
2. Insurance Agent writes a *Policy* or a contract identifying what the insurance company will agree to do when a problem arises for the customer;
3. Customer pays a *Premium* or fee for the policy;
4. When a problem occurs, customer files a claim with the

insurance company;

5. The insurance company reviews the policy to see if the claim is a *Covered Event* or in other words is covered by the terms and conditions of the policy;

6. Insurance company dispatches an insurance *Adjuster* who reviews the situation with the customer and determines what is covered;

7. Adjuster provides analysis to the insurance company and the customer is paid by the insurance company to cover the claim.

Sounds pretty simple but there are many issues that can arise along the way. There is one more term that applies to all insurance policies that we need to understand - the *Deductible*. A deductible is an amount you pay when a problem occurs <u>before</u> the insurance company pays. You pay this deductible <u>each time</u> a problem occurs. For example, let's say you are in an automobile wreck and the damage is estimated at $1,000. If you have a $250 deductible, you pay $250 and the insurance company pays $750. If you have another accident later, you start all over again having to pay the deductible <u>before</u> the insurance company begins paying. What a rip-off you say? I mean after all you have been paying them so much each month, why do they not pay for the whole thing?

Well they would if you have a no deductible but guess what; your monthly payment will be higher with no deductible than with a $250 deductible. Essentially, you are "betting" that you will not have an accident and the insurance company is "betting" you will. The higher your deductible is, the lower your normal monthly payment and the more monthly cash flow you have. Do you want to let the insurance company have your money "just in case" something happens or would you rather control your money? The downside is if you have a problem, you will need some money right away. It is a tradeoff and <u>life is all about tradeoffs</u>. So it is best for you to have a deductible on any policy you have. Determine your deductible based upon your unique budget and cash flow situation and the amount of money that you would be able to obtain in an emergency. All the more reason to do as we discussed previously and save money first to insure (pun intended) you are ready for the unexpected.

You also want to shop around and get quotes from several companies before buying a policy. Be sure the policies from each company are identical so you are not tricked into thinking you are getting a better deal when in fact you are just receiving less coverage. Now let's talk about the types of policies in more detail.

TYPES OF INSURANCE

There are four major types of insurance:
1. Personal Property and Liability;
2. Automobile;
3. Health (usually provided by your employer);
4. Life.

Each type provides coverage for certain situations. You will most likely have policies for each type. We will start by returning to the last chapter and discussing what you need for your new apartment.

PERSONAL PROPERTY AND RENTERS INSURANCE

Up to this point, you have probably been covered by your parent's insurance and do not know very much at all about the subject. First off, you need to realize that the landlord has insurance that covers the building but not its contents. Your lease agreement probably states that you are responsible for obtaining insurance for your belongs and to protect you against any personal liability for negligence that results in properly loss. Whoa – you're blowing my mind you say. Ok, put another way, you need insurance so that if something happens and the apartment burns to the ground and it winds up being your fault, you have insurance to cover you. Conversely, if your neighbor starts the fire, you need to be able to replace your stuff. So how do you know what to get?

The type of insurance you will need is called *Personal Property and Liability Insurance* and is commonly know as *Renter's Insurance*. You can obtain this policy from a variety of sources such as State Farm, Allstate, Prudential or Nationwide. If you or a direct member of your family has served in the military, you can use United Services Automobile Association (USAA) for all your insurance and financial needs. Even if you are not eligible for coverage through USAA, they have a tremendous amount of information about insurance through their non-profit USAA Educational Foundation. You can read more at www.usaaedfoundation.org. You can also find more information about renter's insurance at State Farm's websites http://sfrenters.secureportal.com/ and insurance in general at www.statefarm.com.

The renter's policy will cover you for losses or damage to your personal property. You want to make sure that any personal property insurance covers you for *Replacement Cost* not *Depreciated Cost.* If your property is damaged, Replacement Cost coverage pays you so you can go out and replace that item at its current cost. Depreciated Cost pays you based upon how much the item is worth currently. For example, if your computer is stolen and you bought it 4 years ago, a new computer may cost $1,500 (Replacement Cost) while your computer was only worth $350 (Depreciated Cost). You can see why you want to be sure you have Replacement Cost coverage.

You will also need to determine the *Limits* of coverage or the total amount of value for your property to be sure you have enough coverage to replace your stuff. Take an inventory of all your stuff and add up how much it would cost to replace all of it. You will probably find that you need a limit of about $25,000 for all your personal property (e.g. computer, cell phone, clothes, furniture, TV, stereo, etc.) but you may need more. The insurance agent will help you determine the amounts you need or you can visit the websites I mentioned.

The policy may also cover paying for a hotel room if you suffer a total loss (e.g. fire). It will protect you against any personal liability as well as provide for medical payments for people injured due to your *Negligence* or any situation caused that was your fault. Finally, you can add *Riders* to your policy that provide additional coverage for situations not covered by the "normal" policy (e.g. flood or earthquake). Review the riders carefully and only add them if you are absolutely sure they are required for your situation. For example, you probably would not need an earthquake rider in Atlanta, GA but would not want to have a policy without it in San Francisco, CA.

PERSONAL PROPERTY – HOMEOWNERS INSURANCE

Homeowners insurance provides the same coverage as Renters insurance but it also provides additional coverage for the *Dwelling* or the house itself. This amount will be based upon the appraisal you have done at the time you buy the house and may increase each year due to inflation. The coverage for your personal property is calculated as a percentage (normally 50-75%) of the coverage of the dwelling.

The policy also allows you to include additional liability coverage to protect you should someone be injured at your house. The liability coverage amount is something you determine but in our litigation happy society today it is best to have at least $1,000,000 worth of coverage. This protects you if for instance your dog bites someone or if someone slips in your driveway and break her leg. Riders can also be added to these policies just as on Renters policies to cover your particular circumstances. Your home is a huge investment so do not be cheap when buying insurance but do your homework so you get the best deal.

AUTOMOBILE INSURANCE

Automobile insurance works similarly to Homeowners insurance. You have coverage for the automobile itself and liability protection in case you cause an accident. Each state sets minimum limits for the amount of insurance that must be obtained by a motorist. Unfortunately, some of these limits are too low to cover the "normal" damages that happen in traffic accidents. In addition, some people drive without any insurance at all. For these reasons, the insurance coverage for automobiles is broken down into four types of coverage: Liability, Underinsured Motorist, Uninsured Motorist and Physical Damage.

Liability again covers you if you are at fault in the accident. This includes providing payments for injuries you cause to other motorists or to repair damage to their vehicles or property. The limits of coverage are usually listed in the following manner: *Bodily Injury Each Person – Bodily Injury Each Accident – Property Damage Each Accident.* So, 100-300-100 would provide up to $100,000 to each person injured in an accident, up to $300,000 total for all people injured in an accident and up to $100,000 to repair or replace property that was damaged. Your total insurance premium is based upon the limits of coverage, the age and type of car you drive, how much you drive each year, your driving history/record and where you live. Nevertheless, the higher the limits are that you select, the more your premium will increase. I recommend you have at least 100-300-100 coverage to provide adequate protection for you.

Underinsured coverage makes up the difference if someone else's policy does not have enough coverage for the actual costs incurred by you when the other individual is at fault. *Uninsured* coverage pays from your policy when the individual at fault has no insurance coverage at all. The limits for these types of coverage are usually set to be identical to the liability amounts and should not go below 100-300-100.

Finally, *Physical Damage or Loss* covers your vehicle should it be damaged regardless of who is at fault. It is broken down into *Collision* coverage is for damage to your vehicle or a vehicle you are operating caused by a collision or rollover. You are usually required to have this coverage if you have a vehicle loan. *Comprehensive* coverage pays for damage to your vehicle or any vehicle in your custody resulting from theft of the vehicle, fire, vandalism, flooding, hail, collision with an animal or other perils. It is also usually required if you have a vehicle loan. None of the automobile insurance coverage protects any of your personal property that is in the vehicle from theft or loss. So if you leave your iPod® on the seat and it is stolen, it is not your auto policy that covers the loss, it is your Homeowners or Renters policy but check with your agent to be sure.

You can also have riders attached to the auto policy to reimburse you for towing charges or rental reimbursement should you need a replacement vehicle to drive while yours is being repaired. You may wish to add these if you only have one vehicle or would not have transportation for work or school if you lost use of your car. I have towing coverage through my membership in the American Automobile Association (AAA) which provides additional benefits such as free state maps, TourBook® guides of most major cities and discounts on hotels, car rentals and etc. You must evaluate the benefits available and make the best choice for your situation.

HEALTH INSURANCE

For most of us, health insurance is provided by our employer and in most cases is less expensive than obtaining an individual policy through and insurance company like you do for automobile or personal property insurance. You can generally pick the levels of coverage you want from two to three different levels; an economy plan and mid-range plan the premium plan. These are my terms your provider may use terms like "The A Plan" or "The B Plan" to describe the differing levels. What changes between each level is the annual premium you pay and the amount of deductibles and up front fees you have to pay when you get sick <u>before</u> the insurance pays for everything.

Now health insurance works much different than automobile or personal property insurance. Health insurance has different tiers of coverage regardless of the plan you have selected that become active based upon what you have spent during the year. What level of coverage you are receiving depends upon the amount of expenses you have had during the year. Essentially, the more expenses you have in a given year, the less you have to pay and the more that is covered by the health insurance up to the maximum limits of the policy. Each year, you start over at the beginning of the scale where you have to pay more than the insurance company. It all depends on the type of medical care you need so your best defense is to stay healthy.

The first level of coverage is for the normal visits to your doctor. A *Co-Pay* is an amount of money you pay each time you receive a medical service. Let's say you go to the doctor for a normal annual checkup and the bill is $125. If you have a $30 co-pay, you would pay $30 the insurance company would pay $95. This is totally separate from the next level of coverage which involves your deductible.

With health insurance, your deductible works differently than with automobile or personal property insurance. Your health insurance deductible is an *annual* amount meaning your deductible does not "reset" each time you use your insurance; it is cumulative. Suppose you have a $500 deductible and you visit your doctor in January and incur $300 of deductible expenses. You will have to pay that $300 because you have not met your deductible. In April, you visit the doctor again and you incur $400 of deductible expenses. You must pay $200 more and you have now met your deductible for the year and any other expenses you have are subject to the next level of coverage– your *Out-of-Pocket Maximum*. This is another amount of money you must pay before your reach the highest level of coverage and the insurance company will pay for everything. The Out-of-Pocket Maximum is usually in the range of $1,000 to $8,000 per year depending upon the plan level you have selected and whether you have individual or family coverage.

Once your deductible is met for the year, the insurance company begins paying any claims for service at a certain percentage rate normally 80% until you reach your Out-of-Pocket Maximum. So, for this $400 bill from the doctor, you paid $200 to meet your deductible and filed a claim with your insurance company for the remaining $200. However, now the insurance company is paying at 80% so they will pay $160 and you must pay the remaining $40. If you have a $2,000 Out-of-Pocket Maximum for the year, the amount remaining is now at $1,960. Each time the insurance pays out at 80% and you pay the difference, you are contributing towards your Out-of-Pocket Maximum until you have paid the entire $2,000. Once you have met that limit for the year, the insurance will pay for everything up to the limits of the policy.

Remember, all of these limits are annual numbers so the values reset each year. Therefore, if you are expecting to have medical expenses, it is best to have as many of them occur in the same calendar year so you can get the most benefit from the insurance coverage. Of course you cannot predict when an emergency will happen and you will need medical care. I'm not suggesting you walk around with an unset broken leg until you can accumulate more medical needs. I am advocating that you plan your medical expenses just like everything else and delay *elective procedures*, or treatments that are not a matter of life and death, so you can coordinate when you receive medical services an obtain the most benefits from your policy.

There are also several types of plans that determine which doctors you can use. *Health Maintenance Organizations (HMOs)* are the most restrictive and assign you to a doctor that you must use. *Preferred Provider Organizations (PPOs)* allow you to choose from several doctors in a network so you are more involved in the decision about who will provide you with medical care. *Out of Network* providers are medical professionals who do not have agreements with your particular insurance company and visits to these folks usually cost you more as the insurance company will not pay as much as to HMOs or PPOs.

A final word on medical insurance. Do not **ever** pay for any medical services until a claim has been filed with your insurance company and the insurance company has provided you with an *Explanation of*

Benefits explaining what they have agreed to pay based upon the terms of the policy. Many doctors and hospitals are trying to charge you your deductible up front before you receive service. If you pay immediately and do not wait until the claim is filed, the coordination of payments between the insurance company and your medical providers can get out of sync and you will find yourself having to get a refund from the hospital to be able to pay the doctor (I know because it happened to me). Force the providers to file their claims and wait for their payment.

LIFE INSURANCE

Again, for most of us, life insurance is a benefit provided to you by your employer at an amount equal to your salary. Generally, this is what is called *Term Life,* which means you receive a certain amount of coverage for a set premium. Oftentimes this premium increases as you get older. Other than that, it works much the same way as personal property insurance only it pays a set amount upon your death called the *Death Benefit.*

In general, you should not need life insurance if you are single with no one else depending on you for support. So save the money and invest it somewhere else. Once you get married, have a life partner or start a family, you will want some type of coverage. The *term life* policy offered by your company may be enough and in many cases you can purchase higher levels of coverage (e.g. 2-6 times your salary) at little additional cost. If this is still not enough, you may want to consider some additional coverage.

The other type of life insurance is *Permanent,* which combines a death benefit with "cash value." Part of your premium is diverted into cash value, which is like a savings account maintained for you by the insurance company. This account can help you avoid the need to pay a higher premium as you get older as is often the case with term insurance. The specified period of coverage is usually up to age 95 or 100. You can cancel your coverage and obtain the amount of money in the "savings account" called the *Accumulated Cash Value* although oftentimes there is a penalty for "cashing out" the policy. In addition, you may be able to borrow or withdraw some of your cash value and still keep the policy in effect as long as the premiums are paid.

There are two basic types of permanent insurance: whole life and universal life. *Whole Life*, has three, and sometimes four, basic elements: premium, death benefit, cash value, and sometimes dividends. From the day you buy the policy, you will pay a set premium based on your age at the time of purchase and the premium does not change. So you will pay more in the beginning than you would with a term policy but it will not increase when you get older. One advantage of whole life insurance is that it does not need to be renewed like a term policy that you get from a source other than your employer. As long as you pay your premium when it is due you will have coverage for your entire life.

Another benefit is that the growth in your cash value is guaranteed at a fixed rate and you do not pay income taxes on the amount until you redeem it. You can borrow against the account at an interest rate specified in the policy, which could be lower than the current lending rates offered through banks. Also, you choose when to pay the loan back or you may decide not to repay it. If you die before a policy loan is repaid, the insurance company will normally subtract the outstanding loan amount plus interest from the death benefit. Some whole life policies also pay dividends, which are usually tax-free.

Universal Life is almost identical to Whole Life, however, it is much more flexible so you can customize the policy to meet your specific needs. Another version of Universal Life called *Variable Universal Life* allows you to select the investment vehicle that generates your cash value growth. You can usually invest in stocks, bonds, money market mutual funds, or a combination of the three. Whatever rate your selected investments earn is the rate at which your cash value will accumulate tax-deferred like a 401k plan (which is discussed in Chapter 11). So while you have the reward of potentially higher earnings accumulating tax-deferred, you also assume greater risk. The whole point is to have the cash value account work like an investment account and provide enough returns to pay for the policy without you having to pay from your normal budget. However, be very careful with this type of policy. If the stock market declines, so could your cash value, and you may have to make additional payments to keep your insurance in force.

Insurance is a very useful tool in helping to protect your financial situation. The various policies we've discussed can help you avoid significant expenses when the unexpected happens but do your homework so you get the best coverage for your specific needs.

Chapter 9 - Buying A Car

EVERYONE *loves* that new car smell. Ask any teenager what they want most and they will reply "my own car." Owning your own car is one of the American "Rights of Passage." You feel that you are officially and adult once you've bought that first car. We are drawn to a particular vehicle because of its looks and all the cool features that are offered. I can remember when having a CD player in a car was a serious upgrade yet alone having an audio system capable of interfacing with an iPod®. Many newer models even activate the windshield wipers when it starts raining! However, there are so many more details to consider beyond the looks and options of a vehicle and the process can be quite daunting.

Think about it. Buying a car is one of the few transactions we make that is subject to negotiation. When you purchase a gallon of milk or a loaf of bread, you cannot negotiate the price with the grocery store manager. She would laugh you out of the store. If you decide you want an iPod®, you cannot negotiate the price on Apple's website. You might find a refurbished model for less, but if you but it brand new, the price is what it is. That is not true of a car. The sticker price is only a starting point for what you will actually pay for the vehicle. Several factors including the down payment, trade in value, discounts, incentives and, most importantly, *your ability to negotiate* will affect the actual selling price.

Again, since we do not negotiate often for the things we buy, most of us are not very good at it. We are at a disadvantage from the moment we step on the lot. Why? Because, the guys at the car dealership *negotiate every day for a living!* The only way that you can possibly get a truly good deal is to do your homework, study the information carefully and be prepared to walk away if you are not able to arrive at an arrangement that meets you requirements.

MY FIRST CAR BUYING EXPERIENCE

So let me tell you about the first car that I purchased. First, I did not plan on buying a car the day I did. I was out "looking" simply beginning to make my plans to purchase my first new car. In my naiveté, I was "convinced" to make a purchase *that* day by a pretty good salesman.

Second, since I wasn't prepared and had been convinced that I "must" make the purchase that day, I made some very big mistakes on financing. In fact, since I had *never* taken out a loan in my life, I accepted the rate and terms they gave me as good because they told me it was good (the rate and terms were okay, but I could have done much better).

Finally, since I had not done my homework, I didn't understand that the deal was not as good as it could have been. I actually wound up paying sticker price for the car and not getting the entire value for my trade the way I though I would due to some fancy number manipulation by the dealership.

The information in this chapter should help you do much better than I did when you purchase your first car. We can break the process down into four main steps:

1. Identify the Vehicle;
2. Do your homework;
3. Secure the proper financing;
4. Negotiate the price.

IDENTIFY THE VEHICLE

As I mentioned, there are many factors to consider when purchasing a car. What features do you want to have? Do you want something utilitarian or sporty? Should the car be environmentally friendly or able to tow a trailer? Do you need front wheel drive, rear wheel drive or both? After you have considered all these choices, you then need to see what will fit in your budget. As we discussed in Chapter 6, you can determine how much money you have available for a monthly payment as a starting point. Don't forget to include your annual property taxes and automobile insurance in the total monthly amount. For example, if you have $350 per month to spend on a car, that should include the loan amount plus 1/12 of your annual auto insurance plus 1/12 of your annual property taxes. We will discuss some examples later to explain this further.

To start you research, you need go no further than the Internet. Several sites contain tremendous amounts on information about current cars available and the features and options offered. The sites also provide many articles to help you choose the car that is best for you as well as information about each vehicle's safety and performance. My two favorites are Kelly Blue Book (www.kbb.com) and Edmunds (www.edmunds.com). Go out to the sites and pick 5 to 6 different cars that interest you. Get as much information as you can about them. Then you need to contact your insurance company.

As I mentioned earlier, you will need to factor in the cost of insurance to you total monthly budget. One *very* important note: The amount of insurance you pay (also called the Insurance Rate) varies dependant upon the type of car you purchase and your personal situation. Here's an interesting fact – cars with only 2 seats are more expensive to insure than cars with 4 seats. Why? Simple; most cars with only two seats are "sports" cars. They are designed for speed and have lots of power. The chances of having an accident are much greater in a "sports car" therefore the insurance rate is higher. Other factors that affect the insurance rate are the likelihood that the car can or will be stolen, how much it costs to repair/replace parts after an accident, where you live (i.e. the likelihood that you will be in an accident), how old the car is, how old you are, whether you are married or not, whether you are male or female and etc. So the best thing to do is to narrow down to a few choices and have the insurance company quote you the cost for each one. That does not mean you must pick the least expensive option but you need the information to make the best decision for your budget.

You should also shop for your car insurance and make sure you are getting all the coverage we discussed in Chapter 8. You want to select a firm that has a good reputation and will treat you fairly. Progressive Insurance and AAA are both good choices. You can get a quote on line from either company by selecting the car you plan to insure and the levels of coverage you require. After you have this information, there is another thing you need to know to help you refine your list – what your Personal Property Tax would be for each vehicle you are considering.

Personal Property Tax is a tax assessed each year by some localities for every piece of property owned by individuals. This generally includes cars, motorcycles, boats, homes and airplanes. Not every state and/or locality charges property taxes. You can find out by contacting your local tax office and asking them how they assess the taxes. If they do charge personal property taxes, they will be able to tell you approximately how to calculate the tax on a particular vehicle based upon its value or they will simply provide you with the annual tax amount. You do not need to be completely exact. Just be sure you get enough information to estimate your total annual costs.

Why to you need to do all this financial research as part of identifying the vehicle? Well, remember the budget example in Chapter 4(Page 32)? Let's say your insurance policy is $301.08 <u>every 6 months</u> (insurance is normally billed that way) and your <u>annual</u> property tax is $450. If you *total* monthly car budget is $350, you have to subtract the monthly portions for insurance and property taxes from that amount to determine how much you can afford for the loan payment on your car. So, it looks like this:

Monthly Car Budget	$	*350.00*
Monthly Insurance	$	*50.18*
Monthly Property Tax	$	*37.50*
Total Available for Loan	$	*262.32*

Using that payment, if you had a 7% loan for 5 years, you could afford a car that costs no more than $18,780. This is a big factor in how you choose a car. A $40,000 BMW is out of the question because you simply cannot afford it...yet. So your financial situation affects your car choice options tremendously. Don't worry. There are plenty of really nice cars available for under $20,000. Make a list of all the features that are important to you and be patient – you will find that right car for you.

DO YOUR HOMEWORK

Now, that you have an idea of they type of car you want, here's what you need to know about how to get a good deal. First, every car has a sticker on the window listing all the features and options that are included in the vehicle. The "standard" equipment comes on every car of the same make and model. For example, every 1994 Ford Thuderbird Super Coupe (the first car that I bought) was equipped with a 3.8L supercharged engine. That is included in the basic price for every Super Coupe made by Ford in 1994. The fact that mine had power leather seats for both driver and passenger was an "option" and was listed as such with the additional cost associated with that option. Adding up the price for the standard equipment and all the options gives the total Manufacturers Suggested Retail Price (MSRP) for the car. That's the BIG number in the bottom right hand corner of the sticker on the window so most people refer to it as the "Sticker Price." Now that is not what the dealership paid for it and that is NOT what you want to pay for it. So, what did the dealership pay?

The dealership paid what is called the Invoice Price. This amount the manufacturer (in this example Ford) charged the dealership for the car. Well, almost. This is where it starts to get confusing so pay attention. There is this other amount built into the Invoice Price called the "Dealer Holdback." It is an additional amount (usually 2-4% of the sticker price or invoice price depending on the manufacturer) that is included in the invoice price. Here's the interesting AND confusing part: *the dealer gets that amount refunded from the manufacturer.* The whole process is a bit of a shell game but basically the invoice price is inflated a bit due to how cars are built and sold.

Most of us do not go to the dealer, sit down with a menu, review the options available, make our choices and order our car like we would order dinner at a restaurant. We select from what is already on the lot more like in a cafeteria. The dealer has to purchase all those cars in advance so they are available for us to see. Periodically, the manufacturer provides the dealership with a rebate for "holding the inventory" of cars. This amount is the "holdback" since it is held by the manufacturer to be paid back to the dealership at some point *after* the dealership pays the manufacturer for the vehicle. In most cases, it is refunded quarterly.

All in all it is just one more thing to add complexity to the transaction and confuse most of us into thinking we've gotten a better deal. Perhaps you have seen advertisements for cars where the dealership claims they are selling cars at just $99 over invoice price to save you a lot of money. It's true you save some money but there is another 2-4% they are getting in that deal *above the $99* due to the holdback.

So how do you determine the amount of the invoice price and dealer hold back? In the past it was very, very difficult to obtain this information. There were little black books you could buy that would tell you invoice pricing but not the holdback amount. Now, with the use of the Internet, it is only a few clicks away.

There are two major sites to obtain information about car pricing: Kelly Blue Book (www.kbb.com) and Edmunds (www.edmunds.com). Each site will allow you to configure a car with your desired options and provide you with the MSRP and Invoice pricing for the car. The sites have a lot of other information on them as well and you should spend as much time on them as you need to do "good" homework prior to stopping by the dealership.

Another item to consider is the warranty on the car. Every new vehicle has a warranty that covers any problem you may have with the car for a specified period of time or mileage whichever occurs first and each manufacturer is different. So if you are comparing two different vehicles and they both have similar prices, compare the warranties to see which is better.

Edmunds has a very good article and a detailed table of all the dealer holdbacks at www.edmunds.com/advice/incentives/holdback/index.html. Here's a copy of the holdback table from the site:

Make	Amount of Holdback
Acura	3% of the Base MSRP
Audi	No holdback
BMW	No holdback
Buick	3% of the Total MSRP
Cadillac	3% of the Total MSRP
Chevrolet, GMC	3% of the Total MSRP
Chrysler	3% of the Total MSRP
Dodge	3% of the Total MSRP
Ford	3% of the Total MSRP
Honda	3% of the Base MSRP
HUMMER	3% of the Total MSRP
Hyundai	2% of the Total Invoice
Infiniti	1% of the Base MSRP
Isuzu	3% of the Total MSRP
Jaguar	No Holdback
Jeep	3% of the Total MSRP
Kia	3% of the Base Invoice
Land Rover	No Holdback
Lexus	2% of the Base MSRP
Lincoln	2% of the Total MSRP
Mazda	2% of the Base MSRP
Mercedes-Benz	3% of the Total MSRP
Mercury	3% of the Total MSRP
MINI	No Holdback
Mitsubishi	2% of the Base MSRP
Nissan	2% of the Total Invoice
Pontiac	3% of the Total MSRP
Porsche	No Holdback
Saab	2.2% of the Base MSRP
Saturn	3% of the Total MSRP
Scion	No Holdback
Subaru	3% of the Total MSRP (Note 1)
Suzuki	3% of the Base MSRP
Toyota	2% of the Base MSRP (Note 2)
Volkswagen	2% of the Base MSRP
Volvo	1% of the Base MSRP

Note 1 - Amount may differ in Northeastern US
Note 2 - Amount may differ in Southern US

When calculating holdback, if the holdback is calculated from the:

TOTAL MSRP: consumers must include the MSRP price of all options before figuring the holdback.

BASE MSRP: consumers must figure the holdback before adding desired options.

TOTAL INVOICE: consumers must include the invoice price of all options before figuring the holdback.

BASE INVOICE: consumers must figure the holdback before adding desired options.

As you can see, some manufacturers use the MSRP, some use the Invoice, and some do not have a holdback at all. Some calculate the holdback from the MRSP only including the Standard Options, some from the Total MSRP, and on and on. Wow that's a lot of confusing jargon. Let's try an example with some numbers to show you how it works.

So what car shall we choose? Let's pick one that will not cost a lot to operate day to day (read it gets great gas mileage). We'll pick the Toyota Prius. We'll choose and upgrade package (HK) that includes backup camera, Smart Key system, JBL Premium AM/FM stereo, 6-disc in-dash CD player, MP3 capability, MP3 input jack, Bluetooth, nine speakers, Vehicle Skid Control, security alarm, electro-chromic rearview mirror, Homelink, HID headlamps and front foglamps. We also have a few fees that are included and a Destination Charge. The Destination Charge is on every vehicle and is the cost to get the car to the dealer's lot. We'll use Edmonds to see that the Toyota holdback is 2% of the BASE MSRP (in other words before any options are added). We will also use Edmunds site to obtain the MSRP and Invoice Pricing information:

2007 Toyota Prius 4dr Hatchback
(1.5L 4cyl gas/electric hybrid CVT)

	MSRP	*Invoice*
National Base Price	*$22,175*	*$20,419*
HK Package #4	*$ 3,180*	*$ 2,518*
SET Destination Fee	*$ 55*	*$ 55*
SET Administration Fee	*$ 0*	*$ 610*
Destination Charge	*$ 620*	*$ 620*
Total with Options	*$26,030*	*$24,222*
Net difference (MSRP-Invoice)	*$ 1,808*	*N/A*
Dealer Holdback (2% of base MSRP)	*N/A*	*$ 444*
Net Dealer Cost	*N/A*	*$ 23,779*
Net Difference (MSRP-Invoice-Holdback)		**$ 2,252**

The holdback is 2% of the $22,175 or $444. From the information we gathered we see that the Total MSRP of $26,030 is $2,252 higher than the net dealer cost of $23,779. That means there is $2,252 in the sticker price that you can negotiate. Now, is the actual cost of the car to the dealer is $23,779? Unless you are a Toyota dealer, you will never know for sure. There are so many other factors that affect the actual price a dealer pays to Toyota for this car. However, if you pay close to $23,779 for the car, you know you got a pretty good deal based upon the information we have available. The next step is getting the money to pay for it.

SECURE THE PROPER FINANCING

Now that you know the options you want and the Target Price you should pay for this particular car, how will you come up with the money? There are two main methods to purchase a vehicle if you do not already have the cash in the bank: buying and leasing.

Buying without cash requires a loan for the car. Remember the car loan examples we discussed in Chapter 5? You will need to go to your bank and discuss with them that you are considering buying a car. Tell them you are considering several financing options and you want to determine what interest rate they would offer you. Be sure that you have as much detail about the car or cars you are considering and that you have some idea how long you want to finance the car. Don't forget that the longer the term of you loan, the lower the monthly payment but the higher the total interest and total cash you will pay over the life of the loan.

Your primary concern with the bank or lender is to get the lowest interest rate you possibly can so the monthly payments and total cash paid out are the lowest possible. You want to "shop around" for the best rate but keep one thing in mind – you will get the best rate from someone with whom you have done business in the past. That's why you should start with your bank. If you are keeping your money with them in a checking or savings account, chances are they are interested in doing more business with you. In addition, you could contact AAA and see what they have to offer. The key here is to have your *own* financing arranged *before* you go to the dealership. You want to get the best interest rate possible for the total amount you want to borrow prior to talking with a dealer. That way, you know you will have good loan terms and not be "forced" into whatever financing they have available at the dealership.

You must also consider how much money, if any, you would like to use as a down payment. There is *nothing* that says you must put any money down, however, if you do throw in some cash, you lower the total amount of your loan, the monthly payments and the total money you pay overall for the car. Remember, life is all about trade-offs. You can save that cash and have a higher monthly payment or you can use it to lower the payment but have less cash available in reserve. How do you decide? Simple, do some math and compare a couple of options. Here's an example using our Prius again and assuming we arrived at a negotiated price of $23,925 for the car:

2007 Toyota Prius		
Negotiated Price	$ 23,925	$ 23,925

	Loan Details	
Term in Months	60	60
Interest Rate	6.89%	6.89%
Down Payment	N/A	$ 3,000.00
Net Loan Amount	$ 23,925.00	$ 20,925.00
Monthly Payment	$ 472.50	$ 413.25
Total Payments	$ 28,350.18	$ 24,795.30
Total Interest Paid	$ 4,425.18	$ 3,870.30
Difference	N/A	$ 554.88

Do you understand? You reduce your payment by $60 per month by putting $3,000 down which lowers the Net Loan Amount. That also saves you $554.88 of interest since you are financing less money. So *total* money paid over the life of the loan for the car is less, however, you have to have the $3,000 available at the time you buy the car rather than paying it over 5 years at the rate of $60 per month. Put another way, spending $3,000 cash now saves you ~$110 per year in total money paid for the car. What if you leave that $3,000 in a money market at 4% interest per year?

Year	Annual Interest	Total Saved at 4%
0	N/A	$3,000.00
1	$122.22	$3,122.22
2	$127.20	$3,249.43
3	$132.39	$3,381.82
4	$137.78	$3,519.60
5	$143.39	$3,662.99

Decisions, decisions. If you leave that $3,000 in your high yield money market account, you get $662.99 in interest over the five years. Since you did not use that $3,000 to make a down payment, you need to subtract the $554.88 you would have saved which gives a net of $108. Therefore, after 5 years, the $3,000 in your account has earned enough interest to offset the loan interest with $108 remaining. Don't forget you also have that original $3,000 in the bank as well! Of course this only works if you do not touch that $3,000 for the full five years. We know that a lot can happen over five years that could require the use of that money. If you use it in a down payment, you certainly will not have it available. However, if you use it to buy something frivolous, it will not earn the interest for you. The point is you have to evaluate all your options carefully and make the best decision for you and *your* financial situation.

Leasing is another option. Whenever you see the word lease, think of the word RENT. That is all a lease is – a long term rental agreement. I have only leased one car in my lifetime and I am personally against leases for vehicles. This is for two reasons; you are throwing money away since your payments do not lead to ownership of the vehicle and second because the "residual value" of the vehicle is too much in the control of the dealership. The dealership may try to sell you on this since your "monthly payment" will be so much lower. Let 's look at a lease example on our Toyota Prius:

2007 Toyota Prius

Lease Price	$ 24,225
*Down Payment**	$ 2,258
Term in Months	39
Adjusted Cap Cost	$ 21,967
Monthly Payment	$ 259
*Total Payments**	$ 10,101
*Residual Value**	$ 14,099
Total Price Paid	$ 26,458
Interest Paid	$ 2,233
Effective Interest Rate	**11.43%**

What they tell you is that you will pay only $259 per month compared to our loan payment of $472.50 per month. What they do not make clear is that once you finish the lease term of 39 months, you have to pay an additional $14,099 immediately if you want to keep the car otherwise you turn it over to them. You are also <u>required</u> to make a down payment at the time of purchase in the amount of $2,258. So add the three payments with the * next to them together and you get the Total Price Paid for the car. That equals $2,233 in interest or a 11.43% interest rate. Doesn't seem like a good deal to me at all. Now you can negotiate these deals and change the price a bit but not as much as when buying the car. Also, IF (BIG IF) you believe you will *always* have a car payment and you will not drive your car over the annual mileage limit, leasing could be right for you. After all, always leasing a car means you are most like always going to have a car that is still under warranty so you will only need to worry about routine maintenance (which will discuss a little later in this chapter).

You may be asking, "What does mileage limit mean?" Most leases limit you to a certain number of miles on the vehicle per year. So, if you lease the car for 3 years and you have a 12,000 mile per year limit, you are charged a fee (usually around $0.15 to $0.30 per mile) for each mile over 36,000 on the odometer when the lease is over. Again, it is for these reasons I am not a big fan of leasing but you have to decide for yourself what makes the most sense for your financial plan. Also keep in mind that whether you lease or buy you still must insure the vehicle and pay any taxes that are assessed by your locality.

NEGOTIATING THE PRICE

We have discussed quite a bit of information. You have determined your budget and your *total* car payment each month including insurance and taxes. You have done your homework to determine which vehicles most interest you and fit into your budget. You have secured the financing you need to be sure you can get the best deal. Now it's time to negotiate a price with the dealership.

From the information we gathered, we know how much we want to pay for the car and how much we should pay (invoice – holdback). So go down to the lot. Get to know one of the sales folks and take a test drive. You may drive the car and decide you don't like the way it feels or the way it handles or how it looks from the inside. That's just fine. Above all else – DO NOT RUSH! This is a BIG decision that will be with you for the next 3-5 years depending on the length of your loan. Take the time you need to get it right and be happy with the transaction. If you don't like the first car you drive, shop around. You may have to do homework on another car that you hadn't considered in your preliminary research but "discovered" you like. I cannot stress this enough – TAKE YOUR TIME AND SET YOUR OWN PACE. Buying a car is an emotional experience and you will not do well if you cannot keep your emotions under control.

Another important point to remember is that a car is a *depreciating* asset. That means it loses value over time. Would you be willing to pay the same amount for two identical cars one with 100 miles and one with 10,000 miles? Of course not so be sure you work to get the *lowest purchase price possible.* If you purchase a car and 3 years later you decide to sell it, it will be worth less than what you paid for it. By getting the lowest purchase price possible, there is a good chance that the selling price you set for the car will be more than the amount you owe on your loan. If you do not get the best price, you could be "under water" and have to sell the car for less than what is left to pay on your loan (ouch!).

Let's say you finally find "the" car and you a ready to make an offer to the dealership. They may not accept your offer. Now what? Well don't panic. You can work it out. Just make sure you stay within your budget. You might be saying, "But, I'm not a good negotiator. I can't do this." Well, go find a copy of the book *Getting to Yes* by Robert Fisher and William Ury (look in your local bookstore or you can order it from www.amazon.com). These guys literally wrote the book on negotiating. Reading this book will help you in so many areas of your life. So get it and read it as preparation for your first car purchase. Then go to a yard sale or a swap meet or a local open market and practice. Try to get the merchant to sell you something for less than the price tag on the item. If you mess up here, you're out what a few dollars? And you can *always walk away*. The key is to practice your negotiation skills on small things so you are prepared for something big like the car purchase.

One thing to remember about negotiation – we all like to feel like we got something. To use some economics lingo, we "integrate our losses and segregate our gains." That is just a fancy way to say that losing feels worse than winning feels good. So if you offer $23,779 and they get you up to $23,925 well they got something and you have not moved too far from your initial position. That's negotiating. There may be other alternatives that you can discuss to help them settle on a price with you.

What if the dealership will offer 0% financing? Well, that is fantastic. That is a loan for thousands of dollars without any interest. I once had a 5% loan set up with my bank and had the dealership offer me 1.9% when we negotiated the deal. I accepted their offer of 1.9% but I was very careful to *negotiate the car price first*. You want to get as close to the adjusted invoice price after the holdback is removed to get the best deal. Don't talk about financing with the dealership until you have completed the negotiation for the final price.

Keep in mind another part of the negotiation; IF you accept a loan from the dealership, *they* will make money from the interest you pay. If you get a loan from the bank, the dealership does not make any money on the loan. So if you get "close" to the deal you want, you may be able to convince them to give you a little lower price by using *their* financing. Again, make sure you understand the terms of their loan (interest rate, down payment amount, lengthy of loan, etc) and be sure the monthly payment and total amount of the loan meets your budget *before* you abandon the loan from your own bank. Also be sure you understand any documentation fees, etc prior to signing the deal. The deal is NOT done until you sign the final contract.

Another secret is there are certain times during the year when you are most likely to get a better deal and have more negotiating power. They are at the end of the month, end of the quarter (March, June, September, and December) and at model year change. If you can arrange to shop towards the ends of the months *after* model year change, you could get a great deal on a NEW car that is last year's model. Why? Because the new model year cars are on the lot and the dealer wants to sell all the last year's models. Take advantage of that situation. You still get a brand new car with no miles and for a great price. Who cares that it is last year's model, right? We are most concerned about making sure we meet our budget!

Do not forget about the warranty comparison as well. If the car you choose has a less attractive warranty than one of your other alternatives, you can use that in your negotiation. Discuss that with the dealership and let them know you are considering another vehicle that offers a better warranty and use that to help you get a lower price on their car. It may not work but it is something to consider in the negotiation process.

A final point on negotiation; sometimes, you have to agree to disagree. Fisher and Ury call it "the best alternative to a negotiated agreement." Perhaps you cannot reach a good arrangement. Do NOT settle just to "get it done" or "put it behind you." You *always* have the option to walk away. ALWAYS. NO ONE controls that but YOU! Do NOT be afraid to use it. If you cannot reach terms that meet your budget you MUST keep looking. Patience is the *only* emotion that will help you with your car purchase. Make sure you have plenty of it!

USED CARS

Up to now, we have discussed the process for purchasing a new car from a dealership. But there is a whole other area of vehicle purchases available to you by looking at Used Cars. You could purchase a used car from the dealership. You could purchase a used car from one of the smaller "mom & pop" lots or you could purchase the used car from an individual. But why would you want some one else's "hand-me-down" car? Well, the short answer is that it is a way for you to purchase a *very good* automobile at a price and monthly payment that will be much more suited to your budget.

Now I *know* what your thinking. I don't want to buy a used car. You may be able to afford a new car. In fact several automobile companies including Kia and Hyndai manufacture very good automobiles at affordable prices. But if you have your heart set on a particular model, buying last year's used model or one that is two years old may allow you to get the *exact* car you want without spending quite so much money.

There are also several financial advantages to purchasing a used car. First, you will not be hit with immediate depreciation. What the heck is that? Well, when you go to the dealership to look for that new car, it has a certain value because it is new. As soon as you purchase the vehicle and drive it off the lot, it is no longer "brand new" so it LOSES some of its value or it depreciates. A used car has already gone thru this process so you are not purchasing something that is going to lose value so quickly.

Secondly, you will probably pay less for a *very good* car if you purchase your first one used. When I say less I mean less in both the total money you have to pay and in your monthly loan payment. You can follow all the same steps we discussed in buying a new car to gather information about the used car. To get an accurate amount, you will need to know the mileage of the vehicle and what options are on it. Both KBB and Edmunds provide the price of a used vehicle from that information. They will break it down into three numbers; Trade In Value, Retail Price and Private Party Value.

Trade In Value is the amount someone should expect a dealership to offer if they are trading in the car towards a new car. For someone like you who does not have a car yet, you should look at the Trade In Value as being the same as Dealer Invoice we discussed with new cars except there is no holdback involved at all. So Trade In Value is roughly what the dealership will pay for the car.

Retail Price is what you should expect the dealer to charge you for the car. Now, both of these numbers are estimates. You should still try to get as close as you can to the Trade In Value on the car, however, keep in mind the dealership is there to make money. How do you know how much they paid for that used car? You don't know and there is now way to determine it. Nevertheless, you can assume they will make money on any amount over the Trade In Value. So make them an offer that is 3-4% over the Trade In Value and negotiate from there.

Private Part Value is what you should expect to pay if you purchase from an individual. This amount will be between the Trade In and Retail amounts. This can work to your advantage as you could possibly obtain a car for less than at the dealership. While that can save you money, be EXTREMELY careful. How do you know that the car is not a lemon? If the car breaks 2 weeks after you buy it, what will you do? I recommend that you NOT purchase a car from an individual until you have had experience purchasing a few cars from the dealership.

Remember our discussion about leasing? Dealerships have many, many used cars available that were previously leased by other individuals. Oftentimes, they are designated as Certified Pre-Owned vehicles meaning the dealership has thoroughly reviewed and inspected them before offering them for sale. Many of these cars have the remaining factory warranty still in effect so you are protected if anything did go wrong. These cars are very good choices for first time car buyers and I recommend you limit your first used car purchases to these vehicles or any other used car that has a good portion (at least 50%) of the remaining factory warranty still in place.

Another advantage to owning a used car is that your Personal Property Taxes and Insurance are more likely to be cheaper. All the way around, a used car *can* be a tremendous value. CarMax is a place that has specialized in the used car market. You can shop their store online at www.carmax.com. You can see details about the cars and have an opportunity to review many more different types of cars than you might find at one local dealership. Remember the same rules apply – whether you are at CarMax or the dealership do your homework and make sure you are getting a good deal.

Finally, if you are considering a used car that will NOT have any remaining factory warranty, you will want to have it checked out be a mechanic. This is extremely important since if something goes wrong and you do not have a warranty, you will have to pay for any and all repairs. If you do not know a mechanic, ask some people you trust for a recommendation. This a *very powerful* research tool for any type of service like a mechanic, plumber, electrician, etc. Studies about people's buying experiences indicate that they will only tell a few of their friends and acquaintances when they have a good buying experience but they will tell almost *everyone* when they have a bad buying experience.

Once you have a recommendation for a good repair shop take the car down to them and have them go over the car *before* you buy it. You may have to pay the mechanic but if you discover something major that is wrong it will be well worth the investment. You might also get the seller to agree to pay to have it checked by a mechanic if you agree to give the seller the mechanic's report if you decide not to buy the car. Therefore, make sure you get something in writing from the mechanic that includes the Vehicle Identification Number (VIN) indicating either that everything checked out all right or what items need to be corrected. If the mechanic finds something minor like the brakes need to be replaced due to normal wear and tear or that you need new tires, you can negotiate with the seller to adjust the price somewhat since you would need to pay to get these items corrected. If the seller of the vehicle will NOT agree to let you do this, then you do NOT want to purchase the car they are selling – period. Remember, the key is to be patient and keep your emotions out of the decision process.

A final word about Trade Ins during a car purchase. IF you have a car and you want to purchase another one, the dealership will often accept your car as part of the deal as a Trade In. Remember that you will probably get more selling the car yourself than you will at the dealership. Remember the difference between Trade In value and Private Party value. Nevertheless, if you do trade in your car, be sure not to allow the dealership to roll over any "negative equity" during the deal. Negative equity occurs when what the dealership offers you for your car is LESS than the payoff amount of your loan. The way they get around this is they add it to your new loan for the car you are trying to buy. Quick example; You owe $18,000 on your loan and they offer you $17,000 for your car and a price of $20,000 for the "new" car you are buying. That means you will actually have a loan for $21,000 for your "new" car due to the negative equity being "rolled" into your new loan.

Do NOT let this happen. There are many people in the United States right now that are making HUGE payments on cars that are not worth that much because they have rolled negative equity into their loans more than once. There is no way to recover from this as each time you do it, the situation just gets worse. It is just like charging $1,500 a month on your credit card when you *know* your budget can only support $750. It will catch up with you and the longer you wait the worse it gets. Avoid the negative equity trap!

REGISTRATION, TAXES AND INSPECTIONS

Once you have purchased your vehicle, you will need to get it registered. In order to obtain a registration, you may have to have the car inspected and you may also need to pay your property taxes on the vehicle. These requirements are unique to each locality around the country so how do you determine what you have to do? Simple: find a phone book.

In the front of most phone books, there is information for people who are new to the area including what office or department to contact in order to register a vehicle. You may also find that information online at your county or state website. Another possibility is to use your powerful research skills again and ask someone you know what is required to register the car. Be sure you have done your homework and know how much you will need to spend for all these items. It would be tragic for you to have finally purchased your first car and be unable to afford to register it so you can drive it!

AMERICAN AUTOMOBILE ASSOCIATION (AAA)

The American Automobile Association is a great organization for people who own cars. Here is a little bit about AAA's history from their website:

> The American Automobile Association was founded in 1902 when there were only 23,000 motor vehicles and almost no highways in the United States. The national AAA organization was formed in Chicago by nine motor clubs whose combined membership was less than 1,000 members.
>
> AAA asserted its leadership in the motoring field by promoting better highways and legislation favorable to motorists. AAA's accomplishments have been instrumental in the phenomenal growth of automobile use.
>
> Today, motorists belong to AAA through membership in their local affiliated Clubs. The association consists of more than 47,000,000 members represented in over 75 Clubs in the United States and Canada.

Becoming a member of AAA has many advantages. Immediately upon becoming a member you receive roadside assistance from them 24 hours a day and 7 days a week. If you have any problem with your car, they will send someone to help you. AAA offers a variety of services to drivers including free maps and TripTik® planning guides that you can use to learn more about a particular travel destination including preferred restaurants and hotels. Also, as a member of AAA, you receive discounts at many retail stores as well as discounts on hotel rooms, car and truck rentals and some vacation destinations like Sea World. In addition, AAA offers automobile, home and life insurance policies (as discussed in Chapter 8) at very reasonable rates.

Another special service for their members is their car purchasing service. You tell them the type of new car and options that you would like and they will shop in your area for it and negotiate the best price for you. They can also provide an extended warranty policy for new or used cars. You will need to read over what is covered carefully to see if purchasing one of these policies is right for you. Finally, they have a list of approved automotive repair facilities in your area that they have inspected and certified for their members. They also have their own set of repair shops called AutoMark Car Care Centers that are owned and operated by AAA and AAA members receive a 10% discount off the published repair rates.

There are many, many other benefits they offer as well including Visa and Mastercard accounts. You get all this for an annual membership fee of between $50 and $75. I highly recommend that you become a member of AAA and use as many of their services as possible.

AUTOMOBILE MAINTENANCE

We have discussed how to find and purchase a car and all the benefits of becoming a member of AAA that will help you in that endeavor. Now that you have a car, you have to make sure you keep it in proper working order for two reasons: 1) for the safety of you and your passengers and 2) to insure the vehicle operates properly and you are not left stranded on the side of the road. Even if you have AAA coverage, having your car break down is not fun at all.

So, we need to talk about what things you need to maintain on your car. The main maintenance items on your car fall into these categories:

Lights, Fluids, Routine Maintenance, Tires, and Brakes.

One item you should check regularly on your car is the operation of the lights on the vehicle. Turn on your headlights and make sure both low and high beams work. Make sure the turn signals work both front and rear on both sides. Have a friend hold the brake pedal down and inspect to see that the stop lamps illuminate including the high back brake light. Finally, have your friend put the car in reverse (while keeping her foot on the brake) to make sure the reverse lights operate. The final check is all the interior lights and don't forget the glove box and the trunk. If any of these is not working, replace them or get them replaced by a mechanic.

Once all the lights are operating, the next thing to consider in your maintenance is the fluids for the car. This includes the gasoline, oil, antifreeze, washer fluid, brake fluid and air in the tires (okay, air is actually a gas but go with me here). Each time you fill up the car with gasoline, you can check these fluid levels while the gas is being pumped into the car. There is a dipstick to check the oil level for the car with a minimum and maximum level. You should make sure that it is always *between* these levels. Keep a quart of oil in the trunk so you have it to add when necessary.

You can also check the reservoirs for the antifreeze, washer and brake fluids. The antifreeze reservoir has two levels – Full Hot and Full Cold. If you have driven the car enough that the engine has warmed up (i.e. temperature gauge is in the "normal range"; check your owners manual for details), then the level is okay if it is between Full Hot and Full Cold. Add some more if it is too close to Full Cold. You need to be sure to add the recommended type for your vehicle (again, see the owner's manual) and that it has been mixed 50/50, that is, 50% coolant and 50% water. Most antifreeze can be purchased already pre-diluted like this. The washer fluid should be filled up to the top. The brake fluid has an indicator like the oil dipstick. Just make sure the level is between the MIN and MAX.

Finally, check the tire pressure. You will need a pressure gauge to do this and you can pick one up at any auto parts store. The new digital gauges make it very easy. In addition to being listed in the owner's manual, your car should have a decal in the door frame or on the gas fill door that tells you how much pressure you should have in your tires.

This is the amount of pressure when the tire is cold so make sure to check this *before* you go to get gas. Make note of the pressure in each tire and how much is needed to get to the recommended level. Then, at the gas station, measure the pressure again and add the amount that you recorded when the tire was cold. The reason to do this is that the tire gets hot as you drive and the pressure increases with temperature.

So, for example, let's say the pressure specified for your car is 32 pounds per square inch (PSI) and you measure 28 at home before you go to the station. You need to add 4 PSI. When you measure again at the station, the tire is a 29 PSI. You still must add 4 PSI for a total of 33 PSI in the tire. It will then be at 32 PSI when it is cold. Don't forget to check the pressure on your spare tire as well. If you get a flat that is NOT the time to find out you do not have enough air in your spare tire!

Routine Maintenance covers things that must be done to the car on a regular basis although at different intervals and should be listed in your owner's manual. They include changing the oil and oil filter at the manufacturers recommended mileage interval (normally 3,000 to 7,500 miles), changing the air filter every 12,000-15,000 miles, changing the fuel filter every 10,000 miles and changing the spark plugs every 60,000-100,000 miles. Other routine maintenance items include rotating the tires, front end alignment, checking and replacing the wipers, lubricating the chassis and etc.

One item that is *rarely* remembered on this list is to change the timing belt. The timing belt makes sure that the valves in the engine are in proper timing with the cylinders. If it fails, MAJOR engine damage (read LOTS of money) can occur. So check your owner's manual to determine when the manufacturer recommends changing the timing belt and make sure to get it done within a few thousand miles of the recommended time. If you cannot find that information, call a dealership that sells the type of car you own, ask to speak to their service department and ask them for the interval. Changing that belt can cost from $150 to $300 so be sure you plan for the expense in your budget.

The AAA Automark website has a lot of information about Routine Maintenance at www.automarkcarcare.com/Services/Maintenace. You can learn more about how to perform many of these tasks yourself by searching online. However, if you plan to have the repair shop do them, you should review the costs for these services and put some "extra" savings into your budget so you can pay for them when they are due.

Tires are the next maintenance item to consider and you can check them yourself relatively easily. You want to make sure that you have even wear across the tire. If one side is wearing faster than the other, it is time for an alignment. If the middle is wearing faster than the outside, you are putting too much air in the tires. When it comes time to replace your tires, you should replace them with an equivalent model and type. It is best to do all 4 at once. Tires have a size, speed rating, wear rating, traction rating and temperature rating. Take a look at these pictures:

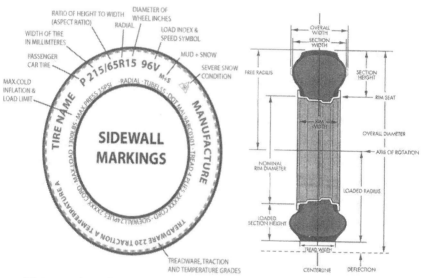

This tire has the letters P215/65 R15 96 V written on it. The P stands for "P-Metric" or some folks say "passenger car." 215 is the width of the tire in millimeters. 65 is what is known as the *aspect ratio* which is a fancy way of saying how high the tire is measured from the inside diameter to the outside diameter. This is calculated by multiplying the tire width by the aspect ratio. For our example it is 215 x 0.65 or 139.75mm. R signifies the tire is a radial tire (most manufactured now are) and 15 indicates the size of the rim diameter in inches. Just be sure to match the size to what you car requires. The size information should also be in the owner's manual or in the door frame where you found the air pressure information.

The number 96 is a code that identifies how much weight the tire can carry (you should not need to worry about this number). Finally a speed rating of V indicates the tire is capable of performing up to *sustained* speeds of 149 mph. Unless you plan on driving regularly at that speed, a lower speed rating on the tire would work fine for you and will be much less expensive.

The Uniform Tire Quality Grade (UTQG) numbers and letters "220 A A" appear in smaller print on the sidewall. The number gives an indication of how well the tire wears over time. A higher number means the tire lasts longer but also means that it is harder and does not handle curves or wet road as well at VERY high speeds. The first letter is for straight ahead braking traction in wet weather conditions. The ratings from best to worse are AA, A, B and C. The second letter is for how well the tire handles the heat generated during driving. The ratings from best to worse are A, B and C. You should by tires that have at least a grade of "A" for each category.

When you get ready to buy tires, you want to find the best deal you can for 4 tires *mounted and balanced* on the car. The tire shop will charge you for the tire, for mounting the tire to your wheels, inserting new valve stems (the things that stick out of the tire where you check and add air) and to balance the tire. Make sure you compare that total cost and not just the cost of the tires. Visit The Tire Rack at www.tirerack.com/about/techcenter.jsp for much more information about tires.

Brakes are something we do not think about until we use them. Changing brakes on a car is not that difficult, however, you do not want to do it yourself unless you know the proper method. If you do not put enough wiper fluid in the car, you cannot spray your windshield. No big deal. If you install the brakes incorrectly, you cannot stop your car. HUGE DEAL! This is definitely something your auto mechanic can do so just make sure you have them checked when you have your oil changed or other services done to the car. Most brakes should not need to be replaced until 50,000 – 60,000 miles. You may have to replace the front brakes more than once before you do the rear brakes since most cars are primarily stopped with the front brakes.

Maintenance of your car is not as difficult as it sounds. You do need to understand some of the basic items I have outlined here and be able to check your fluids and adjust your air pressure in your tires. Beyond that, if you develop a good relationship with a repair shop, you should be confident that any other repairs that need to occur to your vehicle will happen when needed. Nevertheless, you need to have the information to understand what may need to happen and when to be sure you are being treated fairly and that your car is in the best operating order.

Chapter 10 - Owning A Home

OWNING A HOME has always been a big part of the American Dream. There are few feelings that compare to coming home to *your* home that you own. Not someplace you are renting that belongs to someone else but something that is yours. In addition, it is a good financial decision as your monthly payments are helping you build equity rather than just throwing your money away on rent. It is just like the difference between buying and leasing a car. When you buy a car you own the car at the end of the payment term and can sell it and get some of your money back (some because, remember, the value of the car decreases or *depreciates* over time.) But when you lease, you have simply paid for the privilege of using the car and you cannot recover any of the money you have paid. The same rules apply when you buy a home versus renting. The other benefit to owning a home is all the interest you pay on your loan is tax deductible (which is not the case on a car loan). This means you save money in two ways: building equity and reducing your income taxes.

In late 2007, a crisis developed in the home lending industry that had a dramatic affect on our economy. Lenders had gotten greedy and had started issuing loans to people who could not afford them by granting loans to those with poor credit and by qualifying people for loans that were more than they could afford. There were a lot of financing tricks used including interest only payments that allowed the borrower to only pay the interest on the loan for a period of time or Adjustable Rate Mortgages (ARM) which have a lower interest rate for a period of 5 to 7 years and then fluctuate after that (meaning your payment fluctuates as well). Since many people didn't understand what they were signing or didn't care, a lot of people lost their homes. I don't want that to happen to you so I will discuss here the safe ways to go about purchasing a home.

MY FIRST HOME

As I mentioned earlier in the book, I nearly lost my first house because I did not understand everything that was required. In the next few pages I will tell you everything you need to know about purchasing your first home including how to find it, how to finance it, what fees are associated with completing the sale and all the little details that can make home buying very complicated. While I thought I had adequately prepared for my first home purchase, my major mistake was I did not realize that the *closing costs* I had to pay must be paid with a certified check. No personal checks are permitted. *Closing Costs* are the costs associated with buying or selling a home. When you sign the papers, you have "closed the deal" and it is common for everyone from your bank to your lawyer to your realtor to refer to the day you sign the papers as your "closing date." Your closing will usually happen at an attorney's office who specializes in real estate law. There you and the seller will sign papers with witnesses so that the transaction is legal. I had to scramble to get my bank to issue a certified check in time for the closing date and luckily it all worked out! Before you start your home search, you need to have some idea of what you can afford and that includes two things: your down payment and your calculated mortgage payment.

DOWN PAYMENT + MORTGAGE PAYMENT

To determine your down payment and mortgage payment, you first have to decide what type of home loan you want. While there are home loans available that require no down payment, I do not recommend them. The terms and conditions of these loans are very complicated so they should be avoided.

There are two main types of loans I do recommend: fixed rate loans and ARMs. The fixed rate loan is just like it sounds and works much like a car loan and you calculate the payments the same way. The traditional fixed rate home loan is usually for a period of 30 years and requires a 20% down payment. An ARM is a loan that usually has a lower interest rate than a fixed rate loan, however, the rate adjusts at some point in the future usually 5 or 7 years after your first payment. The amount of the down payment can be anywhere from 5-20%. If you believe you will sell your home before the adjustment period begins, an ARM can be a good option since your payments will be less than a traditional fixed rate loan over the same time period. If you plan to stay in the house longer than the ARM period, you should opt for the fixed rate loan.

For a fixed rate loan, I do not recommend a 20% down payment. I have discussed often that it is almost always better to keep your cash in the bank or invested (which I'll discuss more in Chapter 11) than to tie it up in something you are purchasing. I prefer no more than 5% down payment regardless of the type of loan you choose. Also, when you have done the calculations, your monthly payment should be no more than 25% of your NET income each month. Let me explain this in some more detail.

You obtain your loan from a bank or other lending institution the same way that you do for a car loan. The difference with a home loan is that the process requires that you provide the bank with much more information. A home is a much more expensive purchase than a car and the bank wants to be sure you have adequate assets and income to make the payments when they are due. The bank also determines the amount of money they are willing to lend you based upon your *gross* income or your income before income taxes. This can mislead you into thinking you can afford more than you can so that is why I recommend your monthly payment be no more than 25% of your *net* income or your income after income taxes (what most people refer to as your "take home pay").

Let's go back to the example we used in Chapter 5 for the Home Equity loan. The home purchase price was $150,000 and the loan was for a 30 year term at a 6% fixed interest rate. Here is a comparison of two identical loans one with 5% down and one with 20% down:

Mortgage Loan Comparison	5% Down	20% Down
Sale Price of Home	$ 150,000	$ 150,000
Down Payment	$ 7,500	$ 30,000
Net Loan Amount	$ 142,500	$ 120,000
Duration of Loan in Years	30	30
Interest Rate	6.62%	6.00%
Monthly Principle & Interest Payment (P&I)	$ 911.97	$ 719.46
Net Payment Savings	$ N/A	$ 192.51

Now this is where it gets a bit complicated so pay attention. Because you put less than 20% down payment on the house, the bank will require you to have what is called Private Mortgage Insurance (PMI). This insurance is to protect the bank in case you default or, in other words, are unable to pay back your loan. Often times this is a separate payment you make but many banks today will simply charge you a slightly higher interest rate to cover the cost of the PMI. That is the reason the 5% down payment is at a 6.62% interest rate. Once you reach 20% equity in the house (i.e. you have made enough payments that the amount outstanding on your loan is only 80% of the total loan value), you can request to have the PMI removed. If given a choice between a slightly higher interest payment and paying the PMI separately, take the higher interest rate. Remember all your home loan interest is tax deductible but a separate PMI payment is not.

As you can see, your monthly payment is $192.51 less per month when you put 20% down which does save you $69,304 in payments over 30 years. If you put that in a Money Market fund earning 4%, your $192.51 per month becomes $133,000 over 30 years again provided you do not touch it during that time. If you leave the $22,500 you save by putting only 5% down in a Money Market Fund at 4% per year, you will have almost $75,000 after 30 years. So which is better? Depends on your situation. $30,000 is a lot of money to save for a house and can take you a long time. While you are renting and trying to save you are just throwing your rent away and not getting the tax benefits of deducting your loan interest. So the 5% down payment allows you to purchase a home with a lot less money saved and start getting the tax benefits of deducting your mortgage interest that could save you another $30,000 in taxes over 30 years. It is for these reasons I prefer a 5% down payment. However, we still have some more numbers to add to get to your total monthly payment.

INSURANCE AND TAXES

The monthly payment of $911.97 is only the principle and interest payment on your loan. Just like when you purchase a car, you must also include an amount for your monthly homeowners insurance payment as we discussed in Chapter 8. The bank will require you to have insurance since they have given you a loan for the home. You will also need to pay an additional amount each month for your property taxes that your local government will charge you for owning the home. Often times, the bank requires that these amounts be put into an *escrow* account which means they collect payments from you each month for these items and then pay the bills on your behalf.

For this example we will say that your annual homeowners insurance is $625 and your annual property taxes are $1,500. So let's add these to our monthly payments of principle and interest:

Total Monthly Payment
Principle and interest	$ 911.97
Homeowners Insurance	$ 52.08
Property Taxes	$ 125.00
Total Monthly Payment	$ 1,089.05

This is what is referred to as the PITI payment or Principle, Interest, Taxes and Insurance. Multiply this number by 4 (since it should be no more than 25% of your net income) and your "take home pay" should be around $4,400. Better start studying!

You can of course work all this "backwards" to determine the price you are able to pay for a home. Divide your monthly take home pay by 4 to get your 25%. Take that number and subtract an approximate monthly property tax amount and monthly homeowner's insurance amount to determine your available loan payment. Lets work through a quick example. From the information we developed in Chapter 4, we will calculate the purchase price you could afford if you made $30,000 per year *gross* income:

Calculating Total Home Purchase Price

Annual Income	$ 30,000.00
Monthly NET Income	$ 1,764.00
25% of Net Income	$ 441.00
Homeowners Insurance @$625 per year	$ 52.08
Property Taxes @$1,500 per year	$ 125.00
NET Monthly amount available for Loan (P&I)	$ 263.92
Interest Rate	6.00%
Loan Term in Years	30
Total Possible Loan Amount	$ 44,019.09
Down Payment 5% down	$ 2,200.95
Total Possible Sale Price of Home	$ 46,220.04

Now this may look a bit discouraging because using my 25% guideline and with $30,000 per year in income, you can only afford a $46,000 home. Once you look around a bit you will realize there are not that many of those out there. So perhaps your first home is a condominium, which are usually less expensive than a stand-alone house. Your first home may be very small. Regardless, the point is to purchase rather than rent so you can build equity and save towards the next house instead of throwing your money away each month on rent.

If we go back to Chapter 4, I used an example where your rent payment might be about $630 per month and you had $30,000 per year of gross income. If we do our analysis again with these numbers we get:

Calculating Total Home Purchase Price

Annual Income	$ 30,000.00
Monthly NET Income	$ 1,764.00
Total House Payment = Rent Payment	$ 630.00
Homeowners Insurance @$625 per year	$ 52.08
Property Taxes @$1,500 per year	$ 125.00
NET Monthly amount available for Loan (P&I)	$ 452.92
Interest Rate	6.00%
Loan Term in Years	30
Total Possible Loan Amount	$ 75,542.70
Down Payment 5% down	$ 3,777.14
Total Possible Sale Price of Home	$ 79,319.84

Now this may make you feel a bit better that you can afford a house with a selling price of almost $80,000, however, your payment will now be 36% of your take home pay. While I recommend keeping your payment at no more than 25% of your take home pay, you may choose to purchase a home that has a higher monthly payment which would be more than 25% of your pay. I cannot make that choice for you; you have to make the best choice for your unique circumstances. I have provided the tools you need to evaluate all the financial consequences of your decision so you can make the most informed decision possible. However, you should NOT exceed 36% of take home pay for a mortgage payment since you will severely limit your ability to save any money (again, see the Cash Flow examples in Chapter 4).

Finally, you should also look over these numbers carefully and consider how your choice of career may affect your ability to do what you would like with your life. Working for minimum wage somewhere will make it extremely difficult if not impossible for you to save money to purchase a home. You need to be sure to do adequate research about your chosen career and what earning potential you will have based upon your education and experience. Don't misunderstand me; you should not choose a job simply because of how much it pays. Most of the time I have done that in my career I have regretted the decision. However, you do need to completely understand how your career choice will affect your lifestyle and make sure you take action as early in your education as possible to attain the needed skills to acquire the job you want for the lifestyle you want.

LOAN PROCESS

Now that you have some background about how to calculate the loan you can afford, you need to begin shopping for a loan. The first place to start is your local bank or the financial institution you have used for your automobile loan. Make an appointment to speak with someone in their office and tell them you are a first time home buyer and want to see what they have available for 30 year fixed mortgages or a 5-7 year ARM dependant on your circumstances. Do NOT let them talk you into other types of loans. They may run some numbers and tell you that you could afford much more by choosing one of their alternative loans. Well, you are much smarter than that and you now know that they can play many games with the numbers. You control the type of loan you choose.

In order to "qualify" for a loan, you will need to provide them with information about your income, your job, your debts and any other current loans you have. They will perform a financial analysis for you and tell you how much you qualify to borrow. Keep in mind the number they give you may be much higher than what you have calculated you can afford. Although it might be tempting to purchase a home for the amount they have allowed, remember you are making a <u>huge</u> financial commitment here and you do not want them to take the house back from you because you failed to make your payments. Make sure you keep to your budget!

You also want to make sure you get a "Pre Approval Letter" from the institution indicating how much you are qualified to borrow. This is very helpful when you decide to "make and offer" on a house because it lets the seller know you have your financing already arranged.

There are other institutions that offer loans for the first time home buyer. Freddie Mac is a loan company that was established by the Federal Government to assist first time buyers. The Federal Housing Authority (FHA) also offers several programs for first time home buyers. Now, you cannot get a loan directly from these federal agencies. However, your bank or lender may participate in their programs that will help you obtain financing more easily for your first home. Therefore be sure to ask about what loans they have available through government programs or specifically for first time buyers.

You have calculated what you can afford and you have your financing arranged. Let's go find your home!

FINDING A HOME

There are several methods you can use to find a home. You may have seen the little booklets at the grocery store checkout that list homes and land for sale in your area. That is one good source but the easiest way to shop for a home is to use the internet. For example, at <u>www.realtor.com</u> you can select the area of the country you want to search and identify certain parameters about the home that are important like how many bedrooms, how many bathrooms, whether or not it has a garage, etc. Once you enter all that information, the site will search the Multiple Listing Service (MLS) which is a database realtors use to list the properties they are selling. You can also look through your local newspaper for listings as well.

Realtors charge fees for their services helping you find a home. A typical charge is 6% of the purchase price of the home and is usually paid by the seller as part of their closing costs. If you want to use a realtor to help you purchase a home, you want to be sure you have what is called a *Buyer's Agent.* This person is specifically trained to represent the buyer in the real estate transaction (i.e. the home sale) as most realtors are in the business of selling homes. You should interview several buyer's agents and determine which one you think will be the best to help you find your home. Spend some time with your realtor determining the tax rate for properties in your area so you can add those estimates to you loan amount and determine your total monthly payment.

As much as possible, take your time shopping for a home. Make a list of the things that are important to you like the number of rooms, neighborhood, garage, etc. You should also consider the age of the home as an older home is more likely to need repairs before you move in or within a few years after you purchase the home. These are additional expenses you need to figure into your total cost of purchasing the home.

When you select a home, an appraisal will be done on the home to determine the home's value. Your lender will require this to insure that the price you are going to pay for the home is reasonable for the market conditions in your area. The appraiser will visit the house and prepare a report indicating the approximate value of the home for you and the lender. The cost of this appraisal becomes part of your closing costs and will be around $350 but could be more or less depending on your geographic location.

You should also have a Home Inspection performed. Your realtor can help you find a good inspector in your area. Home Inspections cost start at about $350 and can cost much more depending upon the size and value of the home and are also included in your closing costs. The inspector will provide you with a report that will outline the condition of the structure, electrical system, heating and air conditioning, plumbing, and interior and exterior condition. You want to be sure your offer to purchase a home is *contingent* on a satisfactory home inspection meaning if the inspector finds a problem, you are not required to purchase the home.

One additional issue that should be checked is Radon Gas. Radon is a cancer-causing natural radioactive gas that you can't see, smell or taste. You can read more about it at the Environmental Protection Agency's website www.epa.gov/radon/. The inspector installs some simple testing units that remain in the home for a few days and then are sent off to the lab for testing. If Radon is present, you can have a remediation system installed that will eliminate the problem but you should have the seller pay for the installation.

MAKING AN OFFER

Once you have found a home and have a good home inspection report, you are ready to make an offer on the home. Talk with your real estate agent and determine a fair price for the home based upon the current market conditions. Your realtor should perform a competitive analysis that tells you how much similar homes have sold for in the area. Also consider any additional costs you may incur soon after you move into the house. For example, say the home inspection reveals that the water heater may need to be replaced in the next 6 months to a year. You want to deduct the cost of replacing it from the selling price.

Keep in mind that the seller may not accept your first offer. You might be trying to purchase a home for $82,500 that was listed at $91,000. You might receive a *counter offer* from the seller for $87,900. Until you sign that offer, there is no deal. Talk it over with your realtor and determine if the seller's request is reasonable. After all, they have dropped $3,100 off the selling price. Remember to read the book *Getting to Yes* that I mentioned previously. You need to remain focused on your interests and those of the seller to arrive at the best deal. Once you have reached an agreement, you need to prepare for your closing and the associated costs.

CLOSING COSTS

As you may have figured out, purchasing a home is more complicated than purchasing a car. There are many other costs associated with a home purchase that do not exist with a car loan. Total "closing costs" for the buyer are usually 2-7% of the cost of the home. There are specific closing costs that are the responsibility of the seller and other costs that are the responsibility of the buyer. As the buyer, you must be prepared to provide a certified check to cover ALL your closing costs on your closing date.

All the closing costs will be outlined on a United States Department of Housing and Urban Development Settlement Statement also called the HUD-1 form (www.hud.gov/offices/adm/hudclips/forms/files/1. pdf). The closing attorney prepares this form and it identifies who will pay what for each and every cost associated with the purchase. The following table outlines some of the various closing costs and who pays them:

Closing Costs

BUYER	SELLER
Escrow Deposit	*Document Preparation*
Home Loan	*Postage Fees*
Home Loan Down Payment	*Real Estate Commission*
Loan Origination Fee	*State Sales Tax*
Loan Processing Fee	*Recording Fees*
Loan Interest	
Homeowners Insurance	
Homeowners Insurance Reserve	
City & County Taxes	
Title Insurance	
Title Fee	
Attorney's Fee	
Postage Fees	
Appraisal Fee	
Survey Fee	
Home Inspection Fee	
Credit Report Fee	
Tax Service Fee	
Flood Certification Fee	
Recording Fees	
City & County Taxes Refund to Seller	

As you can see, the buyer has many more fees to pay than the seller and you need to be aware of all these fees so you can budget enough money for your first home purchase. Let's talk a bit more about these fees.

Escrow Deposit – This is a down payment you make by personal check at the time you make the offer on your home. It is usually around $1,000 and it simply to let the seller know you are serious about purchasing the home. This money is refunded to you at closing by reducing your overall closing costs.

Home Loan – The amount of the loan you have obtained from the bank.

Home Loan Down Payment – The amount of the down payment you are making towards the house.

Loan Origination Fee – This fee is charged by the bank and can help you adjust your interest rate. This is also called the number of *points* you have paid. So you might secure a loan with the bank for $82,500 at 6% and 1 point or 1% of the loan meaning this fee would be $825. You could pay more points to get a lower interest rate but it requires you to have more money for your closing costs.

Loan Processing Fee – This fee is charged by the bank for the costs they incur setting up your loan.

Loan Interest – Remember Time Value of Money? The bank will charge you interest for every day you have the loan until you make your first monthly payment. Therefore, it is in your best interest to have a closing date as close to the end of the month as possible so you minimize this fee.

Homeowners Insurance – One year of homeowner's insurance cost is paid up front at closing.

Homeowners Insurance Reserve – If you choose to have your homeowner's insurance escrowed, they will charge you 3 months worth of payments at closing for the next year's escrow. Escrow means that the bank collects the money from you each month as it is included in your monthly payment and they pay the bill each year for you. I would recommend NOT escrowing your homeowner's insurance. See if you provider will allow you to pay it directly to them monthly.

City & County Taxes – This is your property tax and you pay the first year in advance. Whether you pay city, county or both depends upon the location of the home. Also, the amount of this tax varies greatly from location to location so be sure to find out from your realtor how much the annual property taxes are <u>before</u> you make an offer on the house so you can see if your total monthly payment fits in your budget.

Title Insurance – Insurance to insure that if there is a problem with your Title that is discovered after closing that the situation can be corrected.

Title Fee – A fee to research the Title to the property and make sure that all transactions concerning the property have been conducted properly in the past and there are no outstanding *liens* or claims of ownership on the property that have not been disclosed by the seller. This is also referred to as obtaining a "clear" title.

Attorney's Fee – Costs from your attorney for preparing everything for the transaction.

Postage Fees – Fees incurred sending documents to various destinations so everyone involved has the necessary information.

Appraisal Fee – Charges from the individual who conducted the Home Appraisal.

Survey Fee – This may be required if there is uncertainty about the property lines of the home or in other words the area of land that is being purchased. This is generally required on a new home but should be on file with the county for older homes and therefore unnecessary unless property lines are in dispute.

Home Inspection Fee – Charges from your home inspector.

Credit Report Fee – Your lender will run a credit report on you (as we discussed in Chapter 5) as part of your loan application process to determine how much money they are willing to lend you.

Tax Service Fee – This cost arises from having your property taxes escrowed or, in other words, paid by your bank. It pays for the service for whomever actually pays your property taxes for the lender each year from your escrow account. The fee is figured into your escrow requirements in the future so you only "see" paying this fee one time at closing. You will most likely not have a choice about escrowing your taxes.

Flood Certification Fee – This is a charge for research that is conducted to determine if the home is in an area that is susceptible to flooding. If it is, you will need additional insurance beyond your homeowner's insurance to protect you specifically from any flooding damage. If at all possible, avoid purchasing a home that is in a flood prone area.

Recording Fees – Various charges for recording the transaction with local government.

City & County Taxes Refund to Seller – Since property taxes are paid as a lump sum annually, the seller has already paid the property taxes for the current year. You have to refund the seller any of the property taxes that have already been paid for the time during the year that you will live in the home. For example, if you purchase your home in September, you owe the seller the amount of the property taxes for October, November and December. This coupled with the interest payment requirements I mentioned earlier make the best time to purchase a home late in the month and late in the year.

The list of fees the seller pays is much shorter and is made up of two primary fees. The *Real Estate Commission* is the amount paid to <u>both</u> the buyer and seller's real estate agents. This fee again runs about 6% of the home value. The other fee is the *State Sales Tax* and it varies from state to state and is similar to any other sales tax charged by the state. The actual list of fees you pay may be different from those I have outlined so just be sure you ask questions and understand why each fee is there before you sign the documents. You can get a list of these fees from your realtor well in advance of making an offer on a home.

This brings us to another interesting financial realization; the down payment is not all you need to purchase a home. I mentioned that the closing costs could be 2% to 7%. If we add that to the 5% down payment, you would need to have, worst case, 12% cash available to "close" on the house. For your $82,500 home, that is almost $10,000. If you recall our example in Chapter 4, you would have around $200 a month in free cash flow. If you put that into a money market account at 4% per year, it will take you around 4 years to save your $10,000. You must understand that you have to manage your money well if you ever want to get out of renting and purchase a home. The only way that you will do this is by establishing your savings targets, setting up a budget and sticking to it.

Chapter 11 - Investing

THE BEST WAY to save your money and have it work for you is to invest it wisely. In this chapter I'll discuss some different methods you can use to invest your money and save for your future. But first, what do you think about when you hear the word investing? Do you think about Wall Street? The stock market? The world of finance is extremely complicated and there are many sophisticated methods you can employ to make your money grow. However, this chapter is not intended to be a comprehensive discussion about every aspect of investing. My desire is to give you some basic understanding of investments as a starting point so the money you save is earning more for you than it would in a simple bank savings account. If you want to learn more than what I outline here, go to your local bookstore and you will find countless books dedicated to the subject of investing. But before you rush off to buy your first investing book, let's cover some of the basics.

An *investment* is anything you purchase that you believe is going to gain value over time. It could be a *stock* that gives you ownership in a particular company. You could purchase a *bond* that is essentially a loan you make to someone else who pays you interest. It could be a *mutual fund* that gives you ownership in many different stocks and/or bonds and has a manager who buys and sells the individual stocks and bonds to reach the target performance for the fund. Or you could purchase a *commodity* like gold or copper (wish I had bought copper in 2004!). Finally, you can purchase a specific item such as a painting or antique. To make sure you are making a wise choice you need to do your homework so you can be certain what you purchase is going to increase in value for you. After all, increasing value is the goal of investing!

TYPES OF INVESTMENTS

Before we talk about some different kind of investments in more detail, we need to refresh our memories about the word *liquidity* from Chapter 4. *Liquidity* describes how easily an asset is converted to cash. Here is a list of assets in order of liquidity from most to least:

Cash ⇒ *Personal Check* ⇒ *Stock/Bond/Mutual Fund* ⇒ *House*

Let's think about it this way. If someone offered to pay you $10,000 for something you did for her, how would you want to be paid? Cash. You have the money and can spend it immediately if needed. If she gives you a check, you have to deposit it in the bank and you have to wait for the check to clear. If she pays you in stock, you have to sell the stock and wait for the *broker* to send you a check that you have to deposit, etc. If you have to wait for her to sell her house before you get paid, it could be longer than 6 months depending upon how long the house takes to sell and how long after that the "closing date" is set.

So, investments have varying levels of liquidity. We will talk about them in order so you can get some understanding of where you would like to place your money. Most times, but not always, the less liquid an asset is, the greater *return on investment* (ROI) or gain in value it provides. There is also a tradeoff between risk and reward. On average, bonds pay less than stocks because stocks are more risky. When you purchase a bond you are paid a certain amount of guaranteed interest for your investment. With a stock, you have no guarantee and you could lose your entire investment, consequentially, the ROI on stocks is generally higher. You must be careful; it is easy to be fooled into purchasing a stock with the expectation that you will make a lot of money only to lose all your money. Let's start out discussing some safer investment options.

INTEREST ACCOUNTS

Interest accounts are any type of account you hold at a bank or financial institution that pays you interest for letting them hold your money. The simplest example is an interest bearing checking account. This is an account that allows you to write checks and pays interest on the money you keep in the account. The amount of money you earn in interest is usually less than 1% and requires you maintain some sort of minimum balance.

Another type of account is a *savings account.* The savings account pays a slightly higher interest rate (perhaps 2%) than the checking account but requires a larger minimum balance. Finally, there is the *Money Market Fund* (MMF). A MMF is type of *mutual fund* that holds several types of *securities* or investments that provide predictable income. You can also look at it as a fancy checking account that requires a higher minimum balance than the savings account (usually over $3,000) but it earns much more in interest oftentimes as high as 4-5%.

You will not get this level of return from a MMF offered through your local bank. The place to go is Vanguard (www.vanguard.com). At the time of this writing, they have a MMF called the Prime Money Market that is paying in the 4-5% interest range for a $3,000 minimum investment. I recommend you save some money and open a MMF with Vanguard as soon as possible. This would be a good place to start putting your money to save for your first house. Keep a checking account with your local bank to pay bills, get cash from the ATM and make sure to have your pay-check direct deposited into your checking account. Then, set up an electronic link between your Vanguard account and your local bank so you can transfer money between the two easily. In fact, you should establish an automatic deposit plan to have a certain amount of money automatically transferred from your checking to your MMF each month. Don't forget the best way to save for your future is to always pay yourself first!

STOCK, BONDS AND MUTUAL FUNDS

The next step on the liquidity scale is Stocks, Bonds and Mutual Funds. A *stock* is an ownership share in a company. In other words, you give the company some of your money in exchange for part ownership in the company. As a part owner, you have a right to vote on issues that are brought before the shareholders for decision such as who the company will use as their accountants. You may also be entitled to a *dividend* which is a periodic payment like interest that the company makes to each shareholder based upon how well the company is performing and how many shares of stock is owned by the shareholder. Finally, because you own the stock, you can gain (or lose) money based upon the value of the stock in "the market".

Stocks are traded in *markets* around the world and the price of each stock is set by supply and demand. The three major markets for stocks in the United States are the New York Stock Exchange (NYSE), the National Association of Securities Dealers Automated Quotation system (NASDAQ) and the American Stock Exchange (AMEX). Stocks are *listed* on one of these three markets and are bought and sold by *traders*. If there is more stock available than people wanting to buy it, the stock price will be lower. If there are more people wanting to buy than there is stock available, the price will be higher. It's simple economic supply and demand. To make money on a stock you have to purchase it when it is low and sell it when it is high. Sounds easy right? Unfortunately, it is not that easy and there are people who spend their entire days studying stocks to try to determine which ones will provide them with the most ROI.

A *bond* is simply a loan that you are providing to someone else. In exchange for your money you are given a guaranteed interest payment on your money or guaranteed ROI. Almost all MMF hold some amount of bonds.

To own a stock or a bond you must first have an account with a *brokerage company* such as Fidelity or Charles Schwab. Brokers are the middleman between companies and investors. To purchase a stock, you would send money to your brokerage company and they would purchase the stock and hold it in an account for you. They charge a fee each time you *trade* or buy or sell a stock. Again, to do well with stocks requires a lot of time and research so if you would like to learn more about how to become a successful trader, take that trip to the bookstore and start doing some research. In the meantime, since you are just starting out, the easiest way for you to begin investing is to put some of your money in a Mutual Fund.

A *mutual fund* is a collection of stocks that is owned by a mutual fund company such as Vanguard. They purchase several different stocks of various companies based upon the goals of the particular fund. This is called *diversifying* which means selecting several stocks so that overall, even as some stocks increase in value and some decrease in value, the overall value of the collection of stocks increases and so does your investment.

For example, if you own a company that makes just trucks you might have a good ROI as long as gas is inexpensive. If gas becomes expensive, the company that just makes cars will have a better ROI since more people will want to drive a more fuel-efficient vehicle and if you own the truck only company, your investment may decline in value. If you own a mutual fund that owns both stocks, regardless of the price of gas, your investment will do better than owning either one alone.

There are many different types of Mutual Funds. Each one invests in particular market segments such as energy, financial, automotive, healthcare, etc. or they may invest in a variety of market areas which is called a *balanced fund*. There are funds designed to generate income through dividends and ones that are designed to increase ROI called *growth* funds and they have increased risk. Let's say you want to own an *aggressive growth* fund or one that is seeking to gain the highest ROI. First, you would need review the information about the various aggressive growth funds offered by Vanguard. To do this you would request a *prospectus* about the funds that interest you. The prospectus tells you all about the fund, its goals, the stocks it owns, etc. You would need to carefully review the prospectus and look at how well the fund has performed in the past (i.e. what is the ROI for the last year, 5 years and 10 years). Once you have found one that you believe will continue to grow in value, you would set up an account with Vanguard and purchase shares of that mutual fund. If you are unsure which fund you should choose, call Vanguard and have them suggest some funds for you to review. Keep in mind that the more aggressive a fund is, the larger the risk and the greater the potential for you to lose money. You also need to understand that just because a fund has done well in the past does NOT mean it will do well in the future.

As an owner of the mutual fund shares, you do not own the stocks themselves so you would not have any voting rights for the individual companies. However, you do have voting rights for the activities of the fund itself and would still benefit from any gains in the prices of the various stocks or any dividends the stocks pay. You also would not pay a fee for every trade you make buying and selling the mutual fund but there is a *management* fee built into the fund that is charged although you never see it. You do not see it because it is figured into the mutual fund share price.

For example, if you owned shares of Vanguard's Wellington fund, there is a 0.27% management fee. So if the published share price of the fund is $31.05, then that is what you would get if you sold your shares. The shares are actually worth $31.05 x 1.0027 or $31.13. Vanguard keeps that $0.08 per share to cover the costs of managing the fund or in other words buying and selling stocks to achieve the target fund performance. You may also be charged an annual account maintenance fee of around $20 if you have less than $10,000 invested in total with Vanguard. Nevertheless, you will do much better investing in a mutual fund than you will trying to keep up with everything that is happening with an individual stock and be much better diversified.

TAXES

Another benefit you receive by purchasing a mutual fund is a reduced tax rate on the income you receive from them. When you sell a mutual fund for more than what you paid for it, the profits are called *capital gains.* Capital gains are taxed at a lower rate than your regular income provided you hold the fund (i.e. buy it and not sell it) for a minimum of 12 months. For example, if you bought 100 shares of the Vanguard Wellington Fund on January 5, 2005 for $30 each and sold them on January 12, 2007 for $34 each, you have made roughly $400 in capital gains. You have to record this as income on your tax return, however, since you held the fund for more than 12 months, the $400 is taxed at a lower tax rate than if you had earned that money in your regular pay check.

You can also use your *losses* from mutual funds to reduce your income tax. Based on the current tax law, each year, you are allowed to deduct up to $3,000 in *capital losses.* If the Vanguard Wellington fund had been at $26 per share when you decided to sell, you would have a $400 *capital loss* that you could record on your income tax as a deduction. Of course we all prefer to receive a gain when we sell but if you have decided that the particular fund you purchased is not performing well, do not risk losing any more of your money; you need to sell. After all a $400 loss is much better than a $3,000 loss and now you know you can use it to reduce your taxes.

Now this special tax benefit only applies to stock and mutual fund gains; any interest you receive from a MMF is taxed as *ordinary income* or at the same rate you are taxed on your paycheck. The capital gains tax benefit is just another reason to consider putting some of your money into mutual funds since you will pay less in taxes on the profit you make provided you hold the fund over 12 months.

TRACKING PERFORMANCE

The performance of each stock, mutual fund and bond can be tracked with online financial sites such Vanguard or for free with sites provided by Yahoo and others. To try this out, just go to http://finance. yahoo.com. In the top left hand corner, there is a spot for you to enter what is called a *ticker symbol*. This symbol is what is used to look up information about a particular stock or mutual fund including how it traded today, the trading trend over time, any news about the company such as new products being released and etc. Try typing in the symbol "AAPL" for Apple Computer and see what you can find out about the company. The internet is a good place to do some preliminary research about your potential investments.

If you know the name of a company but do not know its ticker symbol, just leave the box blank and when you click "GO" there will be a link to help you look up the symbol. Type as much of the company name as you know and then search until you find the correct symbol for that company. See what happens when you type in "Vanguard Wellington Fund."

You may have heard on the nightly news that "the markets were down today and the Dow lost 150 points". WHAT does that mean? Well, in the early days of the stock market, there were no computers. In order to determine how the stock market performed each day, many, many stocks had to be analyzed and their individual performances combined to determine the overall market performance. With all the computations being done by hand, it simply took too long to perform the calculations for the information to be useful. To get a quick sense for how things were doing each day, some performance averages were developed based upon a small number of stocks that represented the entire market. This made it much easier to calculate the daily performance of the market.

The oldest and most popular average is the Dow Jones Industrial Average (DJIA) that was developed by Charles Dow who was one of the editors of the *Wall Street Journal*. The DJIA (commonly called "the Dow") is a collection of the 30 largest and most widely held (meaning owned by the most investors) public companies in the United States. Although it still has the word "industrial" in its name, many of 30 companies in the current DJIA do not provide physical products to consumers but services such as cell phone networks or financial advice. Even though we now have computers that can quickly calculate the performance of the entire market easily each day (which is done by the NASDAQ and AMEX), the DJIA is still used as barometer of the performance of the overall market since its long history has created so much historical data. The historical data allows investors to compare the performance of the market to historical events and evaluate how people are reacting to the current economic conditions.

401K & IRA

A 401k is a retirement plan offered by employers to help their employees save for retirement. An IRA or Individual Retirement Account is another type of retirement account but it is not connected with your employer. Each is an investment account that allows you to choose from a variety of mutual funds to invest in for your retirement. One key thing to remember is that these accounts are for your retirement only. You should not plan to invest money here that you want to access prior to retirement because if you do access the money before retirement, there is a 10% early withdrawal penalty you must pay.

There are three major benefits to a 401k. First, the money you contribute is pre-tax money. That means the money is deducted from your paycheck *before* your income taxes are calculated. This reduces your income and therefore your taxes and actually lets you take more money home while saving than if you did not contribute to the 401k and invested the money with "after tax" dollars. The second benefit is the money grows tax-free. Even if you have your money invested in MMF in the 401k, the interest you receive that would be taxed as ordinary income in a regular investment account is not taxed until you take the money out when you retire. You can also sell your funds and purchase new funds without any capital gains tax. Finally, most employers "match" your contribution up to certain percentage of your pay usually 4%. That means that by simply enrolling in the program, you have given yourself a 4% raise!

The 401k is the primary way to "pay yourself first" and start saving for your future. Review your budget carefully and do your best to contribute whatever is necessary to get your full employer's matching contribution. If your employer doesn't offer a 401k, put money aside for an IRA. Then determine what other money you have available to save and get that into a good MMF for your "regular" savings. Finally, after you have the 401k and MMF growing, start investigating investing in some other mutual funds.

An IRA is funded with after tax money into one of two types of accounts: a *Traditional IRA* or a *Roth IRA*. While there is no employer matching contribution, you still receive the tax benefits of a 401k. Contributions you make to a Traditional IRA can be deducted from your income taxes each year. This is the tax equivalent of making the pre-tax contribution to a 401k and the money in the IRA also grows tax-free. When you withdraw the money in retirement, the "income" you receive is taxed at your income tax rate in effect at that time. Contributions to a Roth IRA are <u>not</u> deductible from your income, however, the money still grows tax-free and is <u>not</u> taxed when you withdraw it since it was taxed when you earned it and made the contribution. So it depends when you want to pay your taxes on the money; when you earn it or when you withdraw it. These are good savings tools to use since they are not connected with your employer. However, should you change employers, you can usually "roll over" your 401k balance into your new employers 401k program or into an individual Traditional IRA without any penalties.

Please be careful. Investing can be dangerous especially if you do not know what you're doing and if you're reading this book, you probably don't. You need to save money. You need to pay yourself first. You've seen the power of compounding interest and you know the sooner you start the better. Investing in the MMF option in your 401k and a non-retirement MMF are both very safe investments that will get you started. While you are contributing to those and building up for the future, go get a copy of the book *Low Stress Investing* by C. Andrew Millard. He does an excellent job of explaining how to go about structuring your mutual fund investing to maximize your ROI and, after all, that is the goal of investing!

Chapter 12 - Family Considerations

MOST PEOPLE do not consider how their choices about family will affect their finances. In the United States we require more instruction and testing to get a driver's license than we do to get a marriage license or have a child. In fact, to get married or have a baby, there is no test you have to take and pass. Be that as it may, each decision you make about brining people into or sending people out of your family has a financial consequence. The events that have the most significant financial affect on us as individuals are marriage and divorce.

Marriage can be a wonderful thing. My parents have been married now for 41 years and both sets of my grandparents were married for over 50 years. When these members of my family got married, people regarded the vow "until death do us part" as a serious commitment. Unfortunately, today people do not take that commitment as seriously. As a result, the divorce rate in the United States has steadily increased over the last 40 years and has settled out in the range of 40-50% for the last decade. Think about it this way; for every two couples getting married this weekend, some other couple is filing for divorce!

In my opinion, this trend is a result of several factors. First, our federal government has continued to increase income taxes and has made it more and more difficult for a single individual to survive. It is next to impossible to have a decent standard of living with only one income unless you have obtained a master's degree. Even then, as an individual, you pay a larger percentage of your pay in taxes than you do when you are married. This is a financial incentive to find a spouse to improve your individual standard of living.

Second, as the "pace" of our society has increased, so has our desire for instant gratification. We are all busy trying to "get things done" and we oftentimes rush into situations without thinking them all the way through. According to the *American Time Use Survey* published by the US Bureau of Labor and Statistics, the average American works 9.3 hours per day. The US Census Bureau publishes an American Community Survey each year and the report titled *Average Travel Time to Work of Workers 16 Years and Over Who Did Not Work at Home* shows that the average commute <u>each way</u> to work is about 25 minutes. Add that to the time spent "at work" and we wind up "working" 10 hours per day. And remember, these are average numbers. Some people spend a lot more time that this working and commuting each day.

Third, the advent of technology has also increased our need for speed. We have phones in our pockets that keep us connected all the time. You can send email anytime from anywhere with your Blackberry. The average television advertisement is no more than 30 seconds long because our attention span does not last much longer than that. Think about this; fast food restaurants such as McDonalds, Taco Bell and Pizza Hut didn't exist until the late 1950s. The first personal computer didn't come along until the early 1980s and it was not nearly as powerful as what you are using today. The hand held cell phone only became ubiquitous in 2003. No wonder we want things fast and most of the advertising you see today is about how to make life easier and get things done faster. We all want to get what we want when we want it without having to wait.

Due to those reasons, I understand how people would get married without carefully considering the potential downsides. After all, marriage brings with it several financial benefits. When two people are married, they combine their incomes while at the same time reducing their living expenses by sharing one home or apartment. Income tax deductions are higher and paycheck withholding rates are lower for married individuals. It's also nice to have someone to help you out buying groceries, doing laundry, cleaning the house, etc. when you have to work 50 hours a week! There are obviously concrete incentives to find that special someone and dive into matrimony.

But remember, 50% of marriages end in divorce. Before you take "the big plunge", consider some of the things you should discuss with your potential spouse.

MARRIAGE

First of all, I am not a marriage counselor. I am not going to tell you how to decide whom you should marry. However, as I mentioned in the beginning of the book, I have been married and divorced twice and those experiences taught me a lot about the financial affects of each. I had always thought that "love conquered all" and because I loved each of my wives very much, I believed each time that I would be married forever. That was how I planned my finances as well and I made some serious mistakes. The only thing I can recommend to you is that you enter in to marriage carefully with a full understanding of what you and your partner want out of life. I'd also recommend some pre-marital counseling so that you can both learn as much as possible about each other and be sure you are making the correct decision.

Most couples do not discuss several important aspects of their lives before they get married. What do you want out of life? What type of lifestyle do you want? Will you both of you work? What about after you have kids? Do you want to have kids? If so, how many children do you want to have? Will you send them all to college? How will you save to pay for college? Will each one get a car when they are old enough to drive? These are just some of the questions that will affect your collective finances so you have to discuss them prior to walking down the aisle.

Keep in mind that "money problems" are one of the top three reasons for relationship problems. What if one of you is a saver and the other one is a spender? How will you reach your financial goals? If you do not make the same amount of money, how will you "merge" your paychecks? Who will pay for what? Again, having these conversations early in your relationship will insure the two of you are making the right decisions together.

I had always believed that when two people got married, they shared everything. After all, that is what my parents had done. I had approached my finances with each of my spouses that way and had set up joint accounts. My paycheck went into the joint checking account and all the bills were paid from it. Looking back now, that is still partially the right decision. However, with the high potential for divorce, there are a few things you can do to insure you protect yourself.

JOINT AND INDIVIDUAL ACCOUNTS

Being married and in love is wonderful. You want to take care of each other and help each other. Establishing joint accounts protects each of you should something happen to the other one. Any joint account you establish should be set up as Joint Tenants With Rights of Survivorship (JTWROS). This means that either of you has the same rights as both of you. If you are the primary earner in the family and you are incapacitated, your spouse can still access all the resources in this account. With JTWROS, if one of you dies, the other can still access the account without having to go through probate court or dealing with the terms of a will which I will discuss a little later in this chapter.

I suggest setting up three accounts: one joint and two individual accounts. You can link them all together electronically and create automatic transfers to fund the joint account. Pay all your bills out of the joint account for things like your car loans, house payment, joint credit card payments, etc. You should set up three credit cards as well. Obtain a Discover Card with both your names as I outlined in Chapter 5 and charge all your daily expenses for groceries, gas, dinner out, trips to Lowe's etc. to it since it pays you 1% back. Remember only charge what you can afford so you can pay it off each month.

In addition, each of you should get your own, individual VISA card. This serves two purposes. First, as I've mentioned, not everyone accepts Discover. Secondly, by having individual cards, you are each establishing your own credit history. This will be helpful to you both should you wind up getting divorced. Pay your individual VISA bills from your individual accounts. As I have mentioned earlier be sure that you get a true VISA card and not a debit card so your account is protected in case the card is lost or stolen.

You should discuss finances with your partner frequently. Make sure each of you understands where the money is being spent each month and how much you have left to save. Be truthful with each other and do not hide anything. If you or your partner starts "hiding" things they are doing with your "collective" money, that is a very bad sign and you need to get back on the same page quickly.

For your savings, you can set up joint accounts for your money market and mutual fund investments. You should keep the individual investment accounts you already have and your spouse should do the same. Decide where you will put the money you save each month (e.g. how much into the joint investment account and how much into your individual accounts). You can also decide to just contribute all your joint savings to the joint account with the understanding that if you divorce you will split that equally between each of you.

Finally, each of you should have an individual 401k with your employer and you should each fund it to the maximum amount allowed to get the employer's match. By federal law, your spouse is entitled to your 401k and if you are divorced, they must sign their rights to it away if you want to maintain full possession of it. That's why you should each have one so that the accounts will be equal. Your IRAs do not have the same ownership rights by your spouse as a 401k. You can designate the individual(s) that will receive the money should you die. These people are referred to as *beneficiaries* and you can designate as many as you wish to split the money however you desire. You can also set up *primary* and *contingent* beneficiaries. If the primary is not still alive when you die the contingent receives the money. For example, many folks designate their spouse as the primary and their children as the beneficiary. Be sure to do this as this keeps the IRA out of probate court as well.

WILLS

A *will* is a legal document that outlines how your affairs should be conducted after you die including such things as who gets your money, who gets your personal possessions and who should care for your children. Upon your death, your will may have to go through *probate* which is the legal process of settling your affairs. In probate, a judge reviews all the relevant information and decides how to settle your affairs. The judge will review the will to make sure it is legal and represents your wishes. In some states there is no probate because, by law, all your assets pass immediately to your spouse without the need for the court's review.

For these reasons, you and your spouse should contact an attorney and each of you should have a will developed. The attorney will help guide you through the process of developing a will that will meet your individual needs. He or she can also give you advice about how you can set up your finances so that if your spouse survives you they will not have to wait for the probate process to access your funds or property. The easiest way to do this is to have all your joint holdings listed as JTWROS but you should discuss your unique situation with an attorney. The attorney fee for developing the will should be somewhere between $300 and $500.

DIVORCE

There are very few things that will happen to you that are worse than going through divorce. Divorce is stressful. It is usually listed along with death of a family member and loss of a job as one of the most traumatic experiences an individual can experience. It is difficult to comprehend how someone who you believed you loved so much could become someone you can no longer have in your life either through his/her choice or yours. Nevertheless, it happens and you need to be prepared for the possibility.

Divorce is very expensive. Attorneys are not cheap and will cost you at least $2,000 possibly as much as $10,000!. You will waste money trying to undo your joint financial situation. Remember all the money you saved by combining expenses and paychecks when you got married? Now you will be establishing two homes, setting up new utilities, and purchasing additional household items such as another washer and dryer and more furniture. No one wins in a divorce and, if you are considering it, I urge you to do your best to work things out with your partner (unless of course you are in a situation where your health or well being is threatened such as physical abuse or drug use). Having gone through it twice myself, it is not a situation I ever want to repeat again. You might want to watch the video located here http://marriageresourcecenter.org/videogallery/4/med/VideoWidget9.htm.

I hope you never find yourself in this position. If you do, again I encourage you to try to work on your relationship and rebuild your lives. After all, if you did your "homework" before you got married, this person you selected for your partner should be willing to work things out. However, in spite of everyone's best efforts, sometimes you cannot resolve your differences. If that happens, you need to prepare yourself for the turmoil headed your way. The best way to be prepared is to have established the individual accounts I mentioned in the marriage section. That way, you can quickly cancel the joint Discover card, move money out of the joint accounts and you will have money in your individual account to get you through. An even better course of action would be to have a pre-nuptial agreement.

A *pre-nuptial agreement* is a legal document that is developed by an attorney that is signed by you and your spouse before you are married. It outlines what will happen should you decide to get divorced. It can be as simple as to say that you all will keep whatever assets you brought into the marriage and split everything that you built together equally. It can also discuss custody arrangements for your children.

Divorce laws vary from state to state so be sure to consult with an attorney to develop the agreement. Some states only have *no-fault* divorce. In a no-fault divorce, regardless of what either party has done (e.g. committed adultery, been physically abusive, been on drugs or alcohol, etc.), _everything_ gets divided 50-50 between you. This is why you need to discuss this with an attorney so you are sure your pre-nuptial agreement will protect you as much as possible.

Again, I hope you never find yourself considering a divorce. They are difficult for everyone involved. Just make sure you make all your decisions carefully and develop a plan before it happens so the experience is as painless as possible.

Final Thoughts

WE HAVE COVERED a lot of information in this book. We've learned everything from how a checking account works to what to consider before getting married. Remember that every choice you make affects your finances from the decision to eat out at lunch today to how much you spend on a gift for a friend. The choices are all yours.

Money concerns can become overwhelming. I know from experience and the financial mistakes I have made in my own life. However, if you manage your money correctly and follow the suggestions I've given you about saving and operating within a budget, you will always have "enough" to live a very good life.

This book is not meant to be the end of your education but the beginning. I have provided you with some very basic information to help you understand how things work and what issues you need to consider when you make your financial decisions. Now it is up to you. You will learn more each time you buy a car, or a house or select the insurance you need. But don't stop there. Use the Internet to learn. Visit the companion website for the book at www.rl101handbook. com. Go to the bookstore and buy books on the topics you do not understand. Realize now that education is something you need to continue throughout your life and just because you do not get "course credit" for learning, you need to continue to seek knowledge. After all, that can never be taken from you.

I recently read the book *A New Earth: Awakening to Your Life's Purpose* by Eckhart Tolle. It is by far one of the best books I have read. Please read it and if you don't understand it, read it again a few years later. The book has taught me that who any of us are as individuals is so much less about the circumstances we experience and endure and so much more about the unique "you" that exists deep inside each of us. Don't ever forget that regardless of what happens to you.

I hope you have found what I have provided in this book helpful and I wish you success in your life and your pursuit of your purpose here in the world.

Acknowledgements

THERE ARE MANY people I wish to thank because of the influence they have had on my life.

First my parents Jane and Rege Duralia. Thank you for your example of love and commitment to each other and your unconditional love and support for me throughout my whole life even at times when I did not believe I deserved it. I know you are always there for me and I am eternally grateful.

My brother David and his wife Jennifer for your support and encouragement especially in the most difficult times in my life and for your example of a truly loving relationship.

My daughter Emily for your unconditional love and your unique light that has brightened my day on so many occasions. I love you dearly and hope your life brings you all you seek.

My first wife Brandy who brought me Emily and taught me what it means to work together as a "financial team" in a marriage. I am grateful that we have maintained such a good relationship for the benefit of our daughter.

My second wife Ellen who showed me that relationships are not always as they appear so life does not always work out the way you think it will regardless of how hard you try.

My best friend from high school Mark Turner who has remained a supportive friend for over 20 years. I have always been able to count on you.

My best friend from college Dave Emmerich who helped me maintain my perspective during so many times in my life. Thank you for showing me another way.

My best friend from graduate school Lon Nebiolini whose advice and counsel has given me guidance throughout my career. You are one of the most grounded individuals I know.

My close pal Pete Berkowitz who has always made me laugh and realize not to take life too seriously. Thanks for showing me that it is never as bad as I may think.

My dear friend Connie Thomas who has counseled me without judgment through some very trying times in my life. Your integrity is unmatched.

My good friends Joe and Mare Ciarlante who assisted me through a very difficult divorce. You have helped me learn how to continue living in spite of adversity.

And finally my teacher Dusty Staub for showing me how to have the courage to dream my dream. Thank you for believing in me.